Pra

"This history of contemporary Christian worship is without rival. It highlights the obvious but also pulls out the obscure elements that shaped today's worship movement. Masterfully researched, this thorough work ensures the powerful forces that shaped the ever-evolving worship movement will be honored and valued."

—Bob Sorge, author, bobsorge.com

"*Contemporary worship* means many things to many people. Some wholeheartedly embrace it; others reject it outright, and over the years, these competing emotional responses have made it nearly impossible to discuss the topic objectively. That is, until now. With a historian's eye for detail and a musician's ear for tone, Swee Hong Lim and Lester Ruth have written a book that fills one of the most significant gaps in worship scholarship today. Meticulously researched, accessibly written, generous in its praise, and balanced in its critiques—this is the book for which many of us have long been waiting."

—Melanie C. Ross, Assistant Professor of Liturgical Studies, Yale Divinity School, New Haven, CT

"In their history of 'contemporary worship,' Swee Hong Lim and Lester Ruth have hit the sweet spot between the academic study of liturgy and a practical guide to understanding and even implementing this form of worship. Particularly useful for teaching is the way Lim and Ruth organize their account by practices of time, space, music, prayer, technology, and scripture. The penultimate chapter on 'The Sacramentality of Contemporary Worship' offers a compelling explanation of why many congregations have found this mode of worship so compelling, while others see it as superficial. This will immediately become a required textbook for the courses I teach on Christian worship."

—Ed Phillips, Associate Professor of Worship and Liturgical Theology and Coordinator of the Initiative in Religious Practices and Practical Theology, Candler School of Theology, Atlanta, GA

"Whether you love, loathe, or ignore contemporary worship, readers will find Lim and Ruth's one-of-a-kind history convincing and rigorous; the authors show how a modern genre of Christian worship claimed its place with structural, musical, sacramental, poetic, ecumenical, multiracial, transnational, and technological ingenuity and why it matters now to consider what it all means and where it is heading."

—Gerald Liu, Assistant Professor of Worship and Preaching, Princeton Theological Seminary, Princeton, NJ

"Swee Hong Lim and Lester Ruth have skillfully researched the roots of contemporary corporate worship: past and present. *Lovin' on Jesus* is an important book for every pastor, worship leader, and worshipper. A big reason for worship methodology getting out of control and becoming the focus of one's worship is ignorance. This wonderfully prepared study will help you keep your worship experience biblically centered, dynamic, and growing."

—Rick Muchow, Founding Worship Pastor, Saddleback Church; worship leader and coach

Other Abingdon Press Books by Lester Ruth
Early Methodist Life and Spirituality
A Little Heaven Below

SWEE HONG LIM & LESTER RUTH

LOVIN'
ON
JESUS

A CONCISE HISTORY OF
CONTEMPORARY WORSHIP

Abingdon Press™

Nashville

LOVIN' ON JESUS:
A CONCISE HISTORY OF CONTEMPORARY WORSHIP

Copyright © 2017 by Abingdon Press

Library of Congress Cataloging-in-Publication Data has been requested.

ISBN: 978-1-4267-9513-8

17 18 19 20 21 22 23 24 25 26—10 9 8 7 6 5 4 3 2 1
MANUFACTURED IN THE UNITED STATES OF AMERICA

CONTENTS

ACKNOWLEDGMENTS

We wish to thank the many people who helped make this book a possibility and enriched its content greatly:

Those who read portions of the text and offered suggestions for improvement including Courtney Tepera, Taylor Burton Edwards, Carrie Steenwyk, Filip De Cavel, Steve Phifer, and Stephen Proctor;

Our conversation partners on Twitter and Facebook who gave us feedback on raw ideas and initial conclusions;

Our editor at Abingdon, Constance Stella, whose enthusiasm for this project from first mention to final manuscript continued to encourage us throughout the writing;

The eighty-plus persons we interviewed as we researched the book, providing insights that enabled us to speak more confidently about the history of contemporary worship;

Our graduate student and research assistant, Adam Perez, whose review of the chapters and their citations was invaluable; and

Our wives, Maria Ling-Lim and Carmen Ruth, whose steady, loving presence continued to cheer us and whose reading of early drafts made the final text a better one.

PREFACE

Is it a contradiction in terms to write a *history* of something that is still called *contemporary*? To call something *contemporary* suggests that it is of the current time, something so "now" that it has no past. Surely having a past is a prerequisite to have someone write a history. But the thing called *contemporary worship* does have a past, even if its name suggests otherwise. For one thing, contemporary worship has been around for half a century, even by that label, and some of its roots can be traced back even further. For another, over that time there have been significant developments in contemporary worship. Contemporary worship in 2017 is not what contemporary worship was in 1977 or 1997. (Feeling the inevitable pull of middle-age nostalgia, we sometimes jokingly tell our students that we want to find a worship leader who can do *traditional* contemporary worship.)

And so, thinking that writing this history is no contradiction at all, we offer to you *Lovin' on Jesus*. We hope to plow a new field with this book. Publications detailing the history of contemporary worship are few; most deal just with the musical aspects of contemporary worship. But telling the history of its music does not tell the full story. Other prior attempts have been case studies. They go deep on a particular example but do not explore the development of a range of liturgical issues over time. And that is exactly what we hope to do: provide a concise history of multiple dimensions of contemporary worship.

We have tried to tell this history well, but we are aware that our pass with the plow of history will be messy. That situation is inevitably the case in fields that have not been tilled before. And so we offer our work humbly, recognizing there will be gaps, omissions, and even—we hope not too many—inaccuracies. Gardeners can tell you that the ability to prepare the soil for planting and harvest increases the more it is cultivated. To break new ground can be difficult. Unfortunately, we are working in a field that is largely untilled. Unlike other topics in liturgical history, ours is not one in which there is a large body of literature from a sizable body of historians. Consequently, we are not stepping into a field that has been worked for years. We are not fine-tuning a history that has been told multiple times.

To tell contemporary worship's history we are appropriating the chapter topics of James F. White's *Introduction to Christian Worship*. Doing so allows *Lovin' on Jesus* to be read as a supplement to his book, providing more information on developments in the last thirty years. Even if our book is read separately, using White's topics provides an excellent general grid to get at the nuts and bolts of contemporary worship as it has developed in a myriad of congregations across America. Chapter 1 defines the term *contemporary worship*, giving its history and the history of alternative labels and thus provides an overall history for this liturgical phenomenon. Chapter 2 discusses the ways time has been a crucial element in contemporary worship. Chapter 3 describes the ways buildings have been used in contemporary worship with a particular emphasis on the history of recent worship technology. Chapters 4 and 5 provide insights into the historical development of music in this way of worship. Chapter 6 explores prayer within contemporary worship, and chapter 7 does the same for preaching and the use of the Bible. Finally, chapter 8 explores the sacramentality of contemporary worship with a special focus given to how God's presence has been experienced and explained.

There is some overlap between our chapters. For example, technology appears in the discussions about both time (chapter 2) and space (chapter 3). Similarly, something about music appears in every chapter, usually with some consideration of music within congregational worship, while technical consideration of contemporary worship's music and songs over time is the focus of chapters 4 and 5.

An observant reader will notice that we have not always replicated the specific content of what White covered under each of his chapter topics. Where his subtopics were germane, we did apply them to contemporary worship. But we thought it would be more useful to allow what was crucial to contemporary worship to dictate the specific contents of each of our chapters.

Readers should observe, too, that we have tried to mirror the approach of White's *Introduction to Christian Worship* in providing basic historical description. Consequently, *Lovin' On Jesus* is not a book telling folks how to do contemporary worship nor do we use it as a platform to either promote or complain about contemporary worship.

As we begin we think it would be useful to discuss the method by which we researched this book. One decision was to recognize music's importance but not limit ourselves to a history of contemporary worship music. Another decision was to investigate contemporary worship as a practice of Christian congregations, not as an abstraction. To that end we have focused on interviewing practitioners, adopters, advocates, and detractors, well-known names and unknowns, from a variety of different size ministries from across the United States and from a variety of ethnic groups (African American, Asian, Hispanic, and Caucasian). Similarly, we have used written materials from these same groups, although, admittedly, materials from white male authors are much easier to find. (We hope this note will be an encouragement for a broader range of practitioners to write and for scholars to do more work in nonwhite expressions of contemporary worship.) We also have sought information from across a range of denominations, seeking especially Lutheran, Methodist, Baptist, Assembly of God, and nondenominational expressions of contemporary worship.

We also decided to not allow our eyes to be drawn only to exceptional or unusual cases, whether by large size or by oddity. It might seem dull to look for the commonplace or everyday, but that was where we could gather the information to tell the history of a liturgical phenomenon that has cut across a wide breadth of churches.

We supplemented our interviews with writings and electronic records pertinent to the history of contemporary worship. Sometimes these writings included books available on the general market, but sometimes they included workbooks from conferences, advertisements, magazines, or newsletters. We have sought out, too, electronic documentation for contemporary worship, especially video or audio of Christians worshipping in the last third of the twentieth century.

And, to keep the topic from spiraling out of control because of its breadth, we have focused on the United States, realizing there are global dimensions to this history that still need to be told.

Finally, a word about our interest in this topic might assist you in knowing what to expect from this book. We both come with our own positive experiences with recent, new forms of worship. Both of us have helped to lead music in contemporary worship. And both of us have been nourished as Christians by it. That gives us a well-disposed posture toward the phenomenon. *Lovin' on Jesus* will thus be a sympathetic history. But we also want it to be a solid history, too. We both bring advanced degrees in liturgical studies—and in Swee Hong Lim's case also in music—which means that we aim for a sound, critical history that can be useful across the church and academia. To that end and with that wish, we invite you, the reader, to begin.

Swee Hong Lim
Deer Park Assistant Professor of Sacred Music, Emmanuel College,
Victoria University in the University of Toronto

Lester Ruth
Research Professor of Christian Worship
Duke Divinity School, Duke University

Chapter 1
WHAT IS *CONTEMPORARY WORSHIP?*

B efore beginning any journey, it is always good to know the path to be taken. And so, before offering a history of contemporary worship, it is good to give some sense of what this book means by *contemporary worship* since this name has come to mean different things. Defining it is necessary, too, because some "contemporary" congregations have never used the term. And other churches have used other labels. Even others reduce the term to a single aspect, usually the musical. Say "a history of contemporary worship" and some hear "a history of contemporary Christian music."

But, by attempting a history of contemporary worship, this book aims for a history of something broader than just the music. We want to tell the story of a multifaceted worship style (to use a term popular with its practitioners) that within the last several decades has come to be an identifiable, widespread liturgical phenomenon.

To provide a better sense of this term and the history of this liturgical development, initially we will address two questions: what is "contemporary worship" and where did it come from? To answer the first question we will describe the observable markers that characterize this new style. When a congregation has worshipped within this style, these are the qualities that normally were present, regardless of whether the worship was labeled "contemporary" or not. Finally, to answer the first question, we will also give a history of the term itself as well as looking at alternative names that have been used.

Where did contemporary worship come from? To answer that second question we will outline the multiple sources that contributed to developing contemporary worship. Like a river drawn from several headwaters and fed by a variety of tributaries, contemporary worship had neither a single point of origin nor solitary influence shaping it. Indeed, the complexity of the phenomenon itself reflects the intricate weaving of impulses and influences that have shaped it.

And so, let us begin our journey.

DEFINING QUALITIES

Take a random group of Protestants and ask them this question: what is contemporary worship? Our hunch is that the answers might be dramatic. Detractors would speak in terms of contemporary worship being the bane of everything that had been good, reverent, and decent in church; advocates would draw a sharply contrasting vision of it being the boon to bring revitalization to the church. Our goal is not to agree with one apocalyptic scenario or the other but to point out that it would be rare to find a Protestant worshipper who does not have some idea of "contemporary worship." That ability suggests contemporary worship has become an identifiable phenomenon, one that has a history. Even though the term itself has been fluid and has its own story, nonetheless the name has become widespread since the 1990s and the phenomenon to which it points even before that. Like a Supreme Court justice once said about obscenity, it might be hard to define but we know contemporary worship when we see it. (Of course, we are *not* saying that contemporary worship is in any way obscene.)

What does one see when looking at this liturgical phenomenon? Generally, whether in recent forms of contemporary worship or their historical antecedents, there have been nine qualities that have tended to characterize the phenomenon. These nine qualities can be organized into four larger groupings. While it is tempting to begin by discussing music because that is the first thing that many think of, let us begin with qualities that were as foundational and, indeed, more critical at one time in contemporary worship's early history.

The nine qualities of contemporary worship, organized into four larger groupings:

- Fundamental presumptions
  - Using contemporary, nonarchaic English
  - A dedication to relevance regarding contemporary concerns and issues in the lives of worshippers
  - A commitment to adapt worship to match contemporary people, sometimes to the level of strategic targeting

- Musical
    - o Using musical styles from current types of popular music
    - o Extended times of uninterrupted congregational singing
    - o A centrality of the musicians in the liturgical space and in the leadership of the service
- Behavioral
    - o Greater levels of physical expressiveness
    - o A predilection for informality
- Key dependency
    - o A reliance upon electronic technology

Those foundational qualities can be gathered under the category of fundamental presumptions. There have been three fundamental presumptions that underline all forms of contemporary worship, including the initial forays in the 1960s. At that time, these qualities were the first features that people often thought of as making worship "contemporary." Contemporary worship today still presumes these qualities even if our consciousness of them has receded as they have transformed into commonplace assumptions. In the 1960s their radical nature was obvious; today we just assume them, even for forms of worship other than contemporary.

The first of these presumptive qualities is the use of contemporary, non-archaic English. Contemporary worshippers expect to worship in language that they use outside of worship. Regardless of the specific act of worship, contemporary worship utilizes current, updated language. That presumption was especially evident in the materials describing contemporary worship in the 1960s. The setting aside of the King James Bible and the dropping of archaic English as the go-to language for Christian worship was the major development that characterized the phenomenon in its earliest expressions. Not surprisingly, this time was characterized by a surge of new translations of the Bible, all aiming for a more contemporary expression of the faith. The goal, whether biblical or liturgical, was not a rejection of distinctive Christian terminology, although that concern occupied some of the early adherents, as much as it was about the level of colloquialism. For worship to be authentic, an important goal, it had to be in the regular language of the people. The updating of worship language was the first and most critical domino that fell in the developments that led to current forms of contemporary worship.

The second presumptive quality is a concern that the content of a worship service be relevant to the contemporary concerns and issues in the lives of worshippers. Since the 1960s, those who designed contemporary worship desired to avoid a to-whom-it-may-concern generality in a service. In the late 1960s that might mean addressing the burning social issues of the day such as tensions about the Vietnam War (as seen in a mime troupe dramatically presenting the trial of war protesters instead of a standard liturgical text); in the 1990s this concern for relevance might mean sermon series based on the pressing felt needs of suburban life; in the 2000s it might mean searching for just the right popular movie clip to set visually and emotionally the theme for a service. And the saga continues. Even as we write there is a flurry of Facebook posts about how churches are utilizing the look and terminology of the latest *Star Wars* movie as the basis for shaping their upcoming Advent and Christmas services.

The desire to address contemporary concerns leads to the third presumptive quality: a commitment to adapt worship to match contemporary people, sometimes to the level of strategic targeting of specific groups. Behind this commitment normally lies the sense of anxiety that inherited forms of worship do not match contemporary people. The regular solution in contemporary worship has been to adapt worship to fit the people, not presume that people should change significantly to fit the worship. Although language and relevance to present-day concerns have been two of the central elements in adapting worship to fit contemporary people, they have not been the only areas in which the desire to adapt has been shown. Updating architecture, leadership style, and technology have been the most common within contemporary worship, not to mention music.

Indeed, updating music has been so important within contemporary worship's history that music has almost become synonymous with the whole phenomenon. Although originally just a part of the cluster of what made worship "contemporary" (language and relevance being the others), music now dominates as the central observable marker of when a church has contemporary worship. Its dominance is not really surprising when one considers music's central role within a contemporary service. Within the history of contemporary worship, there usually have been three aspects of the contemporary nature of the music. Each is a quality that has tended to characterize the phenomenon. Together these three musical qualities create the second large grouping of characteristics in contemporary worship.

The earliest, and first, of the three musical qualities is an intentional use of current types of popular music to provide the musical style for music in worship. Which type of popular music used has varied quite a bit. Contemporary worship services have featured music drawn from a range of genres. The earliest experimentation among youth, for example, used the popular sounds of the 1940s and 1950s, including jazz at a national Methodist youth convention.[1] More commonly folk, pop, and rock sounds have predominated over the history of contemporary worship. Other churches have branched further out, using country and western, hip hop, rap, and bluegrass styles of music. While the sound may be different from church to church, what stays common is the same: fashioning the music of worship to sound like some form of popular music.

This fashioning has shown itself in at least three ways in contemporary worship. One is the instruments used. What instruments a worshipper sees in worship is the clearest clue that the worship will be contemporary. Thus the "victory" of contemporary worship is seen in its instruments: the guitars have beat out the organ.[2] Another way of showing the use of popular music is in replicating a popular sound. In contemporary worship, instrumentalists, vocalists, and the sound technicians usually work to replicate the sound of popular music heard outside the church. Finally, the fashioning after popular music has shaped the nature of the songs themselves in both their lyrical expression (contemporary worship songs tend to be more colloquial than older hymns) and lyrical structure (the use of verses, choruses, and bridges).[3]

Almost as early as the drive for using popular music is the second of the musical qualities to contemporary worship: extended times of congregational singing. In contrast to sprinkling songs one at a time in the order of worship, most contemporary services now allow for a time of extended congregational singing, with several songs following each other. The result has been the entrance of new words into the vocabulary of Christian worship, such as flow

---

1. Thomas E. Bergler's *The Juvenilization of American Christianity* (Grand Rapids, MI: Wm. B. Eerdmans Publishing Co., 2012) is an excellent survey. For a shorter treatment, see Thomas E. Bergler "'I Found My Thrill': The Youth for Christ Movement and American Congregational Singing, 1940–1970" in *Wonderful Words of Life: Hymns in American Protestant History and Theology,* ed. Richard J. Mouw and Mark A. Noll (Grand Rapids: Wm. B. Eerdmans Publishing Co., 2004), 123–49.

2. Michael S. Hamilton, "The Triumph of the Praise Songs: How Guitars Beat Out the Organ in the Worship Wars," *Christianity Today* 43, no. 8 (July 12, 1999): 29–35.

3. Lester Ruth, "How 'Pop' Are the New Worship Songs? Investigating the Levels of Popular Cultural Influence on Contemporary Worship Music," *Global Forum on Arts and Christian Faith* 3, no. 1 (2015), available at http://www.artsandchristianfaith.org.

(how well the songs and the sense of worship transition over time) and set (the list and sequencing of songs). So critical is this time of congregational singing that in many churches *worship* has become a word synonymous with this time, not a word designating the whole service.

The third and last of the standard musical qualities in contemporary worship is in the centrality of the musicians in the service. Part of that centrality is architectural: the space occupied by musicians is usually large with clear sight lines from the congregation to them. Chancels have become stages in many cases, both figuratively and literally, with musicians and band facing the congregation. The musicians are central in terms of time as they tend to occupy the key spot for quite a while given the length of many worship sets, that is, the extended times of congregational singing. Finally, the musicians have a centrality in terms of the role in leadership. Usually there is a key musician known as the "worship leader" who handles much of the service apart from the preaching. Older models of leadership in which nonmusicians (most commonly the pastor or preacher) lead the bulk of the service have been modified or eliminated. In many cases it is difficult for a worshipper to tell who the preacher is until the sermon since the preacher is off stage until then.

Another overarching grouping of qualities that have characterized contemporary worship deals with how people act within a contemporary service. These qualities are behavioral. The first of these behavioral qualities is a higher level of physical expressiveness. People tend to move in contemporary worship, usually in a way that is not totally scripted or overtly directed by those leading the service. People stand, dance, shout, weep, and—in what has become almost a ubiquitous sign of this way of worship—raise their hands. Of course, the amount and kind of physical expressiveness varies between congregations and among different ethnicities, but it is unusual to not find at least some raising of hands in the service.

A predilection for informality is the second of the common behavioral qualities in contemporary worship. One informal dimension is dress. From early expressions in southern California in the 1970s, such as services in which young worshippers came straight from beach to sanctuary, contemporary worshippers have tended to dress down to encounter God. Dressing down affects all involved: preachers, musicians, technicians, and the people in the pews (or on seats, or on the ground, as the case may be). While level of dress in worship (and culture) has drifted generally toward the informal in America over the last half century, contemporary worship seems to have been on the vanguard of the trajectory. And, since people tend to act in ways that correspond to how they are dressed, contemporary worshippers and worship leaders tend to exhibit an overall casualness in worship, too. One reflection of that casualness seen in my congregations is a truly novel development in the long history of Christian worship: widespread snacking during worship. In many contemporary services, people eat and drink, but not the sacrament.

The final quality that characterizes contemporary worship is dependency on electronic technology. To state it bluntly, this dependency has grown so much over the phenomenon's history that it would be rare to find a worship service not deeply reliant upon a machine or even on electricity itself. Indeed, some contemporary worship spaces have been designed so that there is no possibility of natural lighting whatsoever. No electricity equals no light equals no worship. If you take away electricity generally then contemporary worship is hamstrung. This dependency has increased over time and has become pervasive: electricity is needed for planning, playing, hearing, and seeing worship. Contemporary worship unplugged today is not itself.

Nine qualities together define the phenomenon of contemporary worship. While other developments in Christian worship in the last fifty years share some of them, including a number of new forms of Roman Catholic worship, these qualities collectively have given shape to what we know as contemporary worship.

A HISTORY OF THE TERM

A factor that contributes to uncertainty about contemporary worship's history is that churches worshipping in this way have not always used the term. That is true even for a few congregations that have spearheaded the phenomenon's historical development. And so, to finish answering the question about what contemporary worship is, we wish to give a history of the term itself along with looking at alternative names for the same phenomenon.

The term *contemporary worship* saw a surge in use three times in the twentieth century. The first upswing in use occurred from the 1920s through the 1930s. The term did not have a specific, technical meaning in this first upswing. Instead, it became a way of speaking about the worship of a particular people at a certain time and place. Thus contemporary worship could have happened far in the past. (Think medieval Europeans of the eighth century and their "contemporary worship.")

The next surge of usage of the label *contemporary worship* came in the late 1960s through the late 1970s. This upswing actually corresponds to a period of experimentation in worship. One such liturgical experimenter, James White, reflecting on the increased interest in innovation, believed at the time that the period began in the mid-1960s.[4] Some experimenting churches labeled their new services as "contemporary" and announced them as such. Within a couple of years there was a dramatic increase in the use of the term in publications as people wrote about what was happening. This upswing in the term continued the earlier sense of worship of a particular people in a certain time and place. The difference was that the people in mind were the people of today (contemporary people of the 1960s and 1970s) who ought to have worship in their contemporary English addressing their contemporary concerns (remember the social upheavals of the 1960s) and using their contemporary music (that is, music of the 1960s and early 1970s). In the late 1960s, "contemporary" English, relevance, and music made up a kind of trifecta of what makes worship "contemporary."

Updated English was the dominant of the three aspects of 1960s contemporaneity. This sense that being contemporary meant current English parallels the sense of "contemporary" as found in the surge of popular new Bible translations occurring in the same period. But the freshness of worship experimenting was not limited to modernizing English. As stated in one Methodist article in 1971, the chief characteristic of "contemporary worship" was innovation that expressed itself in a variety of ways: "Variety! Continuity! Now sound! Participation! Relationship! Action! and Celebration!" The excitement of experimenting was captured by the exclamation marks found in the original article.[5]

What happened to this initial era of contemporary worship? By the mid-1970s James White was suggesting that many of the liturgical experiments had been absorbed into what many congregations were doing. Since the perspective had become routine, the term had fallen out of use. That was the positive take on the decline of contemporary worship. White also noted a negative reason, too, for the loss of the term in the 1970s: pastors had not experimented well and had worn out congregations. These churches were glad to bid adieu to contemporary experimentation.[6] Many felt a palpable sense of

---

4. James F. White, *New Forms of Worship* (Nashville: Abingdon Press, 1971), 7, 15.

5. Article from the worship subsection of the "Council on Ministries in Your Church" section of *The Interpreter* (March 1971): 24.

6. James F. White, *Christian Worship in Transition* (Nashville: Abingdon Press, 1976), 131–32.

relief that the "far out" services of the 1960s and 1970s were over.[7] To be sure, published usage of the term had decreased by the late 1970s.[8]

But, as we will see, innovating new ways of worship had not come to an end. White's assessment applies largely to mainline congregations. Elsewhere in America, especially in Pentecostal and nondenominational circles, new developments were arising that would have long-term impact and would lead to the rise of the third phase of contemporary worship. Thus the 1970s and '80s, rather than being a time when contemporary worship had ceased, was actually a period of incubation that led to our current, more permanent phase of contemporary worship.

The new worship incubating through the 1980s exploded into widespread awareness in the early 1990s and with it the term *contemporary worship*. By the mid-1990s the term was a clear technical name describing the phenomenon. Since that time the term has spread widely, becoming the most common way to brand, promote, and adopt this new style of worship in mainline congregations.

The term's clear unleashing came in 1994. From that time forward, a deluge of publications followed using it as a technical way to refer to this new form of worship.[9] In these early publications the freshness of the term is shown in a feature that would be anachronistic today: the authors of the feature had to define what the term meant and describe how to get such a service started. Much of this early literature included how-to guides. By 1995 United

---

7. For example, see the feelings of prominent Baptist musician Donald P. Hustad in *Jubilate! Church Music in the Evangelical Tradition* (Carol Stream: Hope Publishing Company, 1981), 332–33.

8. Conclusions about publication rates of words and terms are based on the Google Ngram Viewer, an online tool that charts the frequencies of any word in published books between 1800 and 2008. It can be found at books.google.com/ngrams.

9. Among the first were Timothy Wright's book *A Community of Joy: How to Create Contemporary Worship* (Nashville: Abingdon Press, 1994) and Donald Brandt's *Worship and Outreach: New Services for New People* (Minneapolis: Augsburg Fortress, 1994). Both authors were Lutheran. Wright was a pastor at an innovative Lutheran church in Arizona, Community Church of Joy (now a branch campus of Dream City Church), and Brandt was a member of the national evangelism staff of the Evangelical Lutheran Church in America. From a Pentecostal, Foursquare Gospel church near Seattle, Washington, came a pragmatic videotape by Doug Murren advocating the new style and using the term, titled "How to Design Contemporary Worship Services" (Ventura, CA: Eastside Foursquare Church and Global Net Productions, 1994), videocassette (VHS).

Methodists had their own internally written and published how-to guide for contemporary worship, including workbook and videotape.[10]

By then the term was already in use beyond the content of books. For example, the December 1994–January 1995 issue of the United Methodist clergy magazine, *The Circuit Rider*, was a theme issue dedicated to contemporary worship. Materials from early Methodist adopters show that the term was already being used to market a new style of worship. Lutheran materials from the same period show that the term had already been appropriated by congregations into job titles.[11]

Beyond print, *contemporary worship* became a common term on the lips of pastors, musicians, and worshippers alike. The term quickly gained a breadth and permanency not found in the 1960s. The term had not only emerged in the 1990s as the go-to way of designating a new style of worship but became the backbone for branding and promoting (or rejecting) a new style of worship.

The 1990s adoption of the term *contemporary worship* not only differed from the earlier 1960s upswing with respect to its breadth and permanency but this latter adoption also had a stronger sense of urgency, too. Whereas the 1960s experimentations were concerned with the authenticity of worship—a sense that worship was out of sync with contemporary people—the 1990s explosion of contemporary worship among mainline users retained this drive for authenticity and wedded it to an intrinsic anxiety about declining numbers of worshippers. This worry about the decreasing numeric vitality of their denominations and congregations added a sense of urgency to those who promoted and adopted contemporary worship.

To label the new worship of the 1990s as "contemporary" also became useful to distinguish it from what churches were already doing, that is, traditional worship. Contemporary versus traditional set up a binary utilized by many churches. What labeling a dichotomy of styles allowed many congregations to do was to market themselves as churches where people had choices. (An early synonym for contemporary worship, "alternative worship," highlights this element of options.) Churches hoped such choices would make

10. Cathy Townley and Mike Graham, *Come Celebrate!: A Guide for Planning Contemporary Worship* (Nashville: Abingdon Press, 1995).

11. As found in the article, "Bursting the Barriers: Removing the Roadblock to Contemporary Music," by Dori Collins of Good Shepherd Lutheran Church in Naperville, Illinois, in the Summer 1994 issue of *The Evangelizing Congregation*, a newsletter from the Evangelical Lutheran Church in America's Division of Congregational Ministries. Collins was the Director of Contemporary Worship and Youth Music at her church.

themselves more attractive to both new members and their own parishioners. In a cultural setting where consumer choice was a good, having worship with different styles enabled congregations to see themselves as tolerant and active.[12] The opportunity to self-brand became so useful that many congregations adopted the practice of stamping their contemporary service by its own distinctive, creative name to make it appealing to the potential worshipper.

The irony of this quickly spreading dichotomy was that in the 1990s there actually was not just a simple binary of two styles of worship, even in mainline congregations. Not only were there multiple strands within contemporary worship but there was no monolith of traditional worship. Mainline denominations, in fact, had been implementing liturgical reforms encapsulated in new, official books of worship. While the stylistic veneer might appear similar between what a congregation might have inherited from mid-century, there were deep dissimilarities between that inheritance and what was found in the new denominational resources. The differences came in the lectionary, church year, sacraments, and order of worship. Some of the literature from the 1990s tried to point out the differences among traditional worship but with little success.[13] The perception that there were two ways for Protestants to worship (traditional and contemporary) became entrenched.

And entrenchment over a simple binary of contrast is a sure formula for setting up conflict. And so it was. Almost as soon as the term *contemporary worship* had begun to appear in publications so too writers began to note the "worship wars" being waged in congregations. One of the earliest published users, a Lutheran theologian in 1994, suggested that the worship wars paralleled the broader "culture wars" engulfing the nation.[14] Indeed, bitter disagreements and political machinations spilled across congregations, denominations, conferences, and artistic guilds. The rancor that attended the cultural wars across American society was matched by those engaged in the ecclesiastical variation. While the fighting was often the most intense over musical issues, there were a variety of battle fronts. Christians fought over preaching styles, the use of technology, the impact of popular entertainment,

---

12. See Deborah R. Justice, "Sonic Change, Social Change, Sacred Change: Music and the Reconfiguration of American Christianity" (PhD diss., Indiana University, 2012), 30–32.

13. Examples include Daniel T. Benedict and Craig Kennet Miller, *Contemporary Worship for the 21st Century: Worship or Evangelism?* (Nashville: Discipleship Resources, 1994); Tim and Jan Wright, eds., *Contemporary Worship: A Sourcebook for Spirited-Traditional, Praise and Seeker Services* (Nashville: Abingdon Press, 1997); and Andy Langford, *Transitions in Worship: Moving from Traditional to Contemporary* (Nashville: Abingdon Press, 1999).

14. Ted Peters, "Worship Wars," *Dialog* 33, no. 3 (Summer 1994): 166–73.

the relationship between the pastoral dimensions of worship (Is the service for us?) and its evangelistic ones (Is the service for others?), and even the level of informality and the type of dress appropriate for Christian worship.

Eventually, it seems, the ferocity of the worship wars waned. In some places it appears one side or the other won. In other cases a kind of fusion or hybrid emerged, perhaps beginning with the calls for "blended worship" in the 1990s as well as in congregations that have morphed their worship from one style to another over time. In other cases it appears that congregations simply have slipped into a kind of demilitarized zone with a truce being accepted. The calls for such a truce began in the second half of the 1990s. Perhaps such a truce does indeed exist as suggested recently by the editor of a prominent national magazine.[15] Regardless, contemporary worship by that name has been around long enough that a whole generation of young worshippers and worship leaders do not know of church life without it.

OTHER NAMES

To speak of contemporary worship and its conflict with traditional worship in the worship wars is to speak in a way that is focused on mainline congregations. But the label *contemporary* has not been the only one applied to worship fitting the qualities described above. Go beyond mainline congregations, especially white ones, and you can see how others have used a variety of terms for this liturgical phenomenon. That variety is especially true over time as names grow in favor for a season and then fall out of use.

One different term for contemporary worship has been simply *worship*. The irony is that this term has been the regular name in many of the churches that helped establish *contemporary* worship's basic qualities. *Worship*, for example, has been the regular word in Calvary Chapels and Vineyard Fellowships, two associations of churches that introduced alternative ways of worship in the 1970s and 1980s, as well as in many nondenominational churches that began using a contemporary style of worship.

What stands behind this use of the word *worship* is the sense in the history of these churches that worship's true character had been discovered for the first time. A feeling of having discovered authentic worship fills historical accounts then and since. John Wimber, for example, pastor of the influential Anaheim Vineyard congregation, preached in the late 1970s of discovering what true worship was in the intense, song-driven fellowship of that

---

15. Mark Galli, "The End of Worship Wars," *Christianity Today* 55, no. 3 (March 2011): 5.

congregation's original home group.[16] It was in that group, Wimber said, that God began teaching him how to worship despite Wimber's having been a Christian for over a decade, a staff person at another church, and someone who had helped to establish an institute for evangelism at a large seminary.[17] Those who visited this congregation could report the same sense of discovery of true worship as did Chuck Smith Jr., a Calvary Chapel pastor who stated that prior to participating in the Vineyard worship he could not have "even define[d] worship or describe[d] what it looked like."[18]

This sense of discovery was not limited to California or to the Calvary Chapel congregation. Bill Hybels, for instance, the pastor of the soon-to-be influential megachurch Willow Creek Community Church, was transformed by his experience in a small, charismatic black church in Michigan during the summer of 1982. No longer was just singing words from a page and "going through the motions" of worship enough. Experiencing real worship was about prayers reaching to the soul and longing for an experience of God. Hybels returned to his church in suburban Chicago after that summer and began to instill a sense of this new vision of worship in his staff.[19]

Such accounts of discovering this new sense of worship share several emphases: the importance of congregational singing, the focus in the singing on heart-felt love for God (or Jesus), the criticalness of singing *to* God (or Jesus) and not just *about* God, the full, sincere engagement of the worshipper, and an experience of God during this kind of worship. This combination of emphases stands behind the development of making *worship* and *music* synonymous terms to many worshippers.

Beyond Calvary Chapels, Vineyards, and nondenominational churches, other churches with longer histories spoke of their form of contemporary worship simply as "worship." Assembly of God and Baptist congregations are examples. This labeling of contemporary worship as worship took place

16. John Wimber, "Loving God," in *The Ministry and Teachings of John Wimber* series, CD #303 (Doin' the Stuff/Vineyard Music Group, 2004).

17. John Wimber, "Worship" in "Basic Priorities of Vineyard Christian Fellowship," unpublished ms., Box 13, John Wimber Collection, Regent University Library Archives, Virginia Beach, Virginia, 1–2, 10–11.

18. From a 2005 personal interview found in Charles E. Fromm, "Textual Communities and New Song in the Multimedia Age: The Routinization of Charisma in the Jesus Movement" (PhD diss., Fuller Theological Seminary, 2006), 270–71.

19. Joe Horness, "Contemporary Music-Driven Worship" in *Exploring the Worship Spectrum: 6 Views*, ed. Paul A. Basden (Grand Rapids, MI: Zondervan, 2004), 108, and also Joe Horness, e-mail to Lester Ruth, February 21, 2013.

as these churches morphed all of their congregations' worship into a more contemporary style. Not needing to differentiate among multiple services sorted by style, these congregations could just call what they were doing by the generic "worship" even as this worship might be undergoing massive transformation.

Another widespread term for contemporary worship has been *praise and worship*. Indeed, among Pentecostals and many nonwhite congregations regardless of denomination, this phrase has been the preferred label, and was especially during in the 1980s and 1990s. The term rests upon a distinction made between praise and worship, based on a certain reading of biblical words for worship. As often taught, praise involves recognizing God's actions and attributes and honoring God by recounting these in the third person. Worship comprises a direct affection for the person of God (or, frequently, Jesus Christ as the recipient of worship), expressed in the more intimate language of second person pronouns (The one worshipped is addressed as "you").

Combining praise and worship thus gives a congregation a sense of progress through the extended time of congregational singing. First came praise, which meant songs and brief spoken elements that highlighted divine activity and qualities. The tempos were upbeat and the music reinforced the celebration of God. Then the worshippers would transition to worshipping God. The song tempos would slow and the tone would become more focused on contemplating love for God.

Initially praise and worship was a generic phrase used in a variety of liturgical traditions as a kind of comprehensive term for corporate worship. But a propensity for biblical word studies led Pentecostal authors to start to nuance different meanings for the words *praise* and *worship* in their original biblical Hebrew and Greek. The distinction was made by the late 1970s and became more widespread in Pentecostal teaching materials in the mid-1980s. Books based on the distinction between praise and worship appeared as how-to guides. Many authors supplemented studying biblical word meanings with biblical typologies through which certain objects or texts provided models for how to put praise and worship songs together to create flowing song sets leading to a sense of entering into God's presence. Types based on the different passages and areas of the Old Testament tabernacle or temple were especially common. In the late 1980s Integrity Music's bimonthly praise and worship music tape subscription service reinforced the term in popular usage.

Thus, although its origin and main use was in Pentecostal circles, the term *praise and worship* was picked up by other white Protestants, especially before the turn of the century. The magazine *Reformed Worship*, for example, dedicated a whole issue (Number 20, June 1991) to explore the rise of a contemporary style of worship under the label *praise and worship*.

Seeker-driven, seeker-sensitive, and related terms were other labels referring to contemporary worship in the 1990s. At the time these terms were widespread but have since fallen out of favor. Especially used by ministers influenced by the Chicago-area megachurch, Willow Creek Community Church, a seeker-service label highlighted a central quality of contemporary worship: a desire to adapt worship to match contemporary people to the level of strategic targeting. That tactical use of worship characterized Willow Creek's approach at the time, especially in its weekend services aimed at the unchurched.[20] Thousands of churches sought to follow Willow Creek's lead as the rationale for implementing a contemporary style of worship. (At the time Willow Creek and some churches following its pattern would not have labeled seeker services as "worship" per se. Nonetheless these services fit the qualities of contemporary worship as described above.) Many appropriated the seeker-related language used by Willow Creek and other groundbreaking megachurches at the time. Over time the terms have fallen out of widespread usage, especially as Willow Creek has transformed its sense of worshipping and making disciples in recent years.

Modern worship has been another term that has had a good degree of use. Music executives coined the term *modern worship music* intentionally in the late 1990s to have a way of promoting worship music that was an edgier style of rock, much of it originating from outside the United States.[21] Modern worship was contemporary worship that used this new music. Thus the term became another way of differentiating between worship styles, but the point of contrast was not so-called traditional worship but existing types of contemporary worship that used the earlier style of contemporary worship music known as praise choruses or praise and worship music. Modern worship has never had the same extent of circulation as has had either contemporary worship or praise and worship.

The intentional coining of a new way to label contemporary worship hints at the creative impulse within the phenomenon. Despite the centrality and permanence of the term *contemporary worship*, a babel of names for the

---

20.   See Lester Ruth, "*Lex Agendi, Lex Orandi*: Toward an Understanding of Seeker Services as a New Kind of Liturgy," *Worship* 70, no. 5 (September, 1996): 386–405.

21.   Monique Ingalls, "Transnational Connections, Musical Meaning, and the 1990s 'British Invasion' of North American Evangelical Worship Music," in *The Oxford Handbook of Music and World Christianities*, ed. Suzel Reily and Jonathan Dueck (Oxford: Oxford University Press, 2016), 425–48.

contemporary services circulated as the twenty-first century began. In addition to those mentioned above, popular literature on worship used labels based on internal qualities of the service (linear, organic, creative, indigenous, or authentic), targeted age group (boomer, buster, gen-X, or millennials), or technological dependence (multisensory or multimedia).[22] This range does not even take into account the fusion of worship styles known as "blended" or in the rise of "emerging worship" after the turn of the century.

THE SOURCES OF CONTEMPORARY WORSHIP

Having looked at the qualities of this style of worship and its various names, it is appropriate to wonder where this worship came from. As noted earlier, this liturgical style has never been a monolithic phenomenon, either in its origins or developments. It had several points of origin as well as followed several intertwining paths of evolution. Each of these points has supplied something to the DNA of the phenomenon and has shaped its various manifestations over time. Adjust the relative influence of each of these contributors and you get the variety of expressions of contemporary worship.

One early contributor to contemporary worship was a set of developments in youth ministry starting in the mid-twentieth century. At that time Christians absorbed what had become a widespread cultural attitude that the future lay with the young. It became self-evident that institutions concerned about their future needed to look to the younger generations. As it was true for the nation so it was true for the church. This perspective was soon wedded to a sense of urgency underlying a necessity to change as ministries noted youth's disinterest. The rallying call soon became, "We are in danger of losing the youth if we do not meet them where they are." Pairing the importance of youth to the urgent propriety of meeting their interests created a strategy of targeting in youth ministry. "We have to figure out what speaks to the youth," many thought. And so many youth ministries began to adapt aspects of church life, including worship and especially worship music, to target the desires and interests of youth.

---

22. See Lester Ruth, "A Rose by Any Other Name: Attempts at Classifying North American Protestant Worship," in *The Conviction of Things Not Seen: Worship and Ministry in the 21st Century*, ed. Todd E. Johnson (Grand Rapids: Brazos Press, 2002) 33; reprinted in *American Theological Inquiry* 2, no. 1 (2009): 85–104.

The results have been numerous and widespread, leading to what one scholar calls the "juvenilization" of American Christianity.[23] Generational thinking became common in how churches approached their ministries. Once generational subgroups can be defined, then ministry can be targeted at them. Planners became experienced at experimenting in order to create an attractive and interesting worship experience. A propensity for adapting, with a particular emphasis upon musical style, turned into an element weaving its way through many forms of contemporary worship.

Liturgically this youth-related point of origin also has meant that youth and college-age ministries have provided a seedbed for new developments in contemporary worship. Over the years many practices that first emerged in worship targeted for teenagers and young adults became more widespread as that generation turned older and more powerful. For example, many mainline early adopters of contemporary worship in the 1990s had developed a taste for guitar-led, informal services in which they had participated in youth and college ministries in prior decades.

Another source for contemporary worship was Pentecostalism. This Protestant liturgical tradition emerged at the beginning of the twentieth century as a revisioning of a New Testament emphasis upon the active presence and ministry of the Holy Spirit in Christians. The revival of the Azusa Street Mission in Los Angeles beginning in 1906 was an important threshold for the tradition's emergence and spread. The historical hallmark has been in promoting a distinct experience of being filled or baptized with the Holy Spirit, evidenced by speaking in tongues. Pentecostals scoured the New Testament for other lists of spiritual gifts (*charismata*). The result in worship was a liturgical tradition that was expressive and exuberant. Over the twentieth century Pentecostalism experienced periods of its own internal renewal, including one in mid-century (the Latter Rain Movement) that seems to have awakened several practices and teachings that eventually would have an impact on contemporary worship.[24] Aspects of Pentecostalism's piety and practices entered into other churches through charismatic renewal movements that began in the 1960s.

Pentecostalism's shaping of contemporary worship has been both through its own internal developments and through an influencing of other

23. Bergler, *The Juvenilization of American Christianity*. Bergler's description of this history is helpful.

24. Scholarly liturgical research on this movement is frustratingly sparse. But see Bill Hamon, *The Eternal Church*, rev. ed. (Shippensburg, PA: Destiny Image Publishers, 2003), 225–38.

Protestants in worship piety and practices. A first point of shaping has been in mainstreaming the desire to be physical and expressive in worship. Indeed, a picture of worshippers with hands raised has become the ubiquitous image of contemporary worship (not to mention evangelicalism itself). Contemporary worshippers with hands raised and faces lifted should thank the Pentecostal teachers whose work noting the physicality of biblical words for worship established a sense of the propriety for such expressiveness. A second point of influence is related: highlighting intensity as a liturgical virtue. This inner motivation is what leads to the outward physical expression. Whether expressed as intimacy or passion, intensity became the sought after goal in contemporary worship.

Pentecostalism also has brought a certain expectation of experience to the forms of contemporary worship, which is a third point of influence. Simply put, Pentecostalism contributed contemporary worship's sacramentality, that is, both the expectation that God's presence could be encountered in worship and the normal means by which this encounter would happen. But this contribution was not about redefining the sacraments of baptism and Communion but reshaping an understanding of God's people praising and worshipping, especially as these people sang. What emerged was a sacramentality of music or corporate song expressed in biblical texts such as Psalm 22:3, where God is said to inhabit, dwell, or be enthroned upon the praises of God's people. This biblical rooting of the liturgical expectation for encountering God, active and present through the Holy Spirit, molded how the extended worship sets were to be viewed. In the early days of contemporary worship, a set was not just about having opportunity to sing songs; it was a journey of being ushered into the presence of God.

A musical sacramentality raises the importance of the worship set as well as the musicians leading this set, which is the fourth point of broader influence of Pentecostalism on contemporary worship. This development has fused with a liturgical democratizing that has sometimes occurred in traditions with a strong emphasis upon the Holy Spirit, like Pentecostals. Since God is no respecter of persons in the sharing of the Spirit, these traditions at times have deemphasized the role of distinct clergy in leading worship. The result that has shaped much of contemporary worship has been in making musicians the main worship leaders, not pastors. In most of Christian worship those with responsibility for preaching and sacraments were the worship leaders, although in contemporary worship that has not been the case. Musicians, including one who is designated as *the* worship leader, have central roles in the worship space and in leading acts of worship. This centrality can be seen, too, in the evolution of church staff positions where musicians have gained new names (worship pastor) and responsibilities (having the most creative hand in developing the service).

Developments in youth ministry and Pentecostalism have not been the only sources for contemporary worship. Contemporary worship has been shaped by the baby boomer generation. This generation, made up of Americans born immediately after World War II through the beginning of the 1960s, began to come of adult age in the second half of the 1960s. Not coincidentally, this time coincides with the first experimentations with contemporary worship by that name, as noted above.

The common characteristic of baby boomers was a questioning of tradition. Just because something is old does not make it right. Just because something has been inherited from the previous generation does not give it value. And just because something has been promoted by a human institution does not make it legitimate. These perceptions easily led to a certain kind of liturgical iconoclasm through which traditional liturgies became suspect in a search for new forms of worship that seemed more authentic.

Indeed, authenticity as determined by the worshippers became an underlying ethos throughout contemporary worship: whatever worship is, it must be "true to us." Thus the propriety to create new forms of worship became self-evident as creativity itself became another fundamental element of contemporary worship's ethos. "Sing to the Lord a new song" (Ps 96:1) became a common motto for the entire phenomenon. This desire to sing a new song—not an old song—to the Lord comes not just from finding that sentiment in the Bible but in a cultural sense of what seems naturally true and right.

One critical outlet for the drive for authenticity has been the role of music for baby boomers as a marker of individual and social identity. In the midst of incredible social turmoil in the late 1960s, baby boomers used musical choice as a way of claiming identity.[25] Music told people who they were and to whom they belonged. To choose a style of music was a way of declaring what your values were.

The effect on contemporary worship's history has been twofold. Along with Pentecostal teachings on the importance of praising God, this social role for music has reinforced the significance of music generally—and the popular-based aspects of this music specifically—in contemporary music. All contemporary worshippers have thought, "I must sing my music." The other effect on contemporary worship has been to contribute to the likelihood of

---

25. Hamilton, "The Triumph of the Praise Songs," 30.

worship wars when commitments to different styles of worship music came into close contact.

One group among the baby boomers, the Jesus People, has had an especially strong influence on contemporary worship.[26] The Jesus People movement arose as a Christian element in the hippie counterculture of the late 1960s. As with this hippie counterculture, many of the first Jesus People were on the West Coast of the United States. However, Jesus People were soon found across the nation, and their perspective became mainstreamed into larger evangelicalism with events like Explo '72, a multiday event with teaching, worship, and a music concert held in Dallas, Texas, in June 1972. By the late 1970s the visible distinctiveness of this Christian counterculture had faded, although the movement's impact has lingered, especially seen in the origins of contemporary worship.

A main influence of the Jesus People in the development of contemporary worship was being a major source for contemporary worship music. Many of the songs that would become favorites of the 1970s and 1980s in contemporary worship came from young Christians within the movement. Classic contemporary worship songs like "Seek Ye First" and "Father, I Adore You" are examples. Beyond the songs, the Jesus People helped establish the guitar as the primary instrument of contemporary worship, too. And they also helped institutionalize the processes to distribute a steady stream of new songs through publishing houses focused on disseminating the new worship music. Maranatha! Music and Mercy Publishing were among the first.[27]

The piety of the Jesus People has had an influence on contemporary worship too. The informality of dress and casualness of leadership that marked early Jesus People meetings have spread throughout the larger church. And note the name for the movement: they were the Jesus People, not a generic God people. There was an intense focus on Jesus Christ as Lord and Savior that awakened and reinforced a longstanding evangelical affection for him as the object of worship, a sentiment often found in the lyrics of contemporary worship songs.[28]

---

26. Larry Eskridge's *God's Forever Family: The Jesus People Movement in America* (Oxford: Oxford University Press, 2013) is the best general overview. See the book's final chapter for a summary of the movement's ongoing impact.

27. Their history can be found in Robb Redman, *The Great Worship Awakening: Singing a New Song in the Postmodern Church* (San Francisco: Jossey-Bass, 2002), 55–56.

28. Lester Ruth, "Some Similarities and Differences between Historic Evangelical Hymns and Contemporary Worship Songs," *The Artistic Theologian* 3 (2015): 70, available at http://www.artistictheologian.com.

Another main source for the development of contemporary worship was the mid-century development of church growth missiology. Originating as an examination by Donald McGavran of why certain missions grew and others did not, he and others applied this missiological inquiry to America starting in the 1960s and '70s. Sociological explanations arose on why some churches grow and others do not. In the popular literature coming from church growth proponents, descriptions about the qualities that attend growth easily transitioned into prescriptive principles that churches desiring to grow should adopt. These principles appealed in the 1980s and '90s to mainline denominations and their pastors who grew ever more anxious about their declining membership.

What the church growth movement has contributed to the rise of contemporary worship is a motivation for many to adopt this new style of worship as a way to make and keep members more effectively. Church growth thinking reawakened a liturgical pragmatism that has characterized much of American Protestantism since the branding and promoting of camp meetings in the Second Great Awakening at the beginning of the nineteenth century. The mind frame is thoroughly American because of its democratic and capitalistic assumptions about numerical validation. Those assumptions create a liturgical pragmatism driven by numbers: What works to produce the greatest numbers in worship? When fused with evangelistic concerns, the perspective creates an approach to worship that assesses worship from the outside in: What works best in worship for the people who are not here and are not members already? In many cases strategically thinking pastors merged this pragmatic approach to worship with a suspicion of inherited, "traditional" forms of worship. If these older forms do not work well, many wondered, are we not free as air (to use the words of nineteenth-century evangelist Charles Finney) to find what does? For many pastors and congregations, especially in the heady days of the 1990s, what seemed to work was adopting contemporary worship. Creativity and innovation became self-evident virtues.

Although earlier church growth literature did not feature liturgical considerations, by the 1990s many church growth authors did. They highlighted large churches with dramatic increases in membership as well as a contemporary style of worship. Thus C. Peter Wagner, a well-known church growth advocate, noted that contemporary worship was nearly universal in congregations like Willow Creek Community Church, which he labeled "the new apostolic churches."[29]

---

29. C. Peter Wagner, ed., *The New Apostolic Churches* (Ventura, CA: Regal Books, 1998).

Beyond just being described in writing, many of these churches offered conferences and educational materials that gave congregations eager to adopt contemporary worship a template and tools for doing so. Our interviews with early mainline adopters of contemporary worship show that these conferences and materials gave many a way to start contemporary services in the 1990s. Mainline denominational evangelism or youth departments likewise resourced congregational efforts to implement contemporary worship as did some ecclesiastical leaders. Denominationally affiliated publishing houses also began to supply resource materials for those wanting to adopt contemporary worship for strategic, evangelistic purposes. Abingdon Press was a leader in this work, publishing in the 1990s at least eleven books with "contemporary worship" in the title.

THE OVERARCHING DEVELOPMENT

Note that all of these points of origin and influence for contemporary worship emerged in the mid-twentieth century. While it would be possible to trace aspects of contemporary worship's typical makeup to earlier tendencies in Protestant worship—the early Salvation Army's adoption of then radical music for evangelistic purposes—contemporary worship's roots are in a confluence of developments arising in midcentury and coalescing.[30] It was not only American culture that was shook up in this decade but the church's worship as well.

Looking at the entire phenomenon from a bird's eye view, it is possible to describe an overarching development of contemporary worship. The 1960s was a cultural environment in which several factors combined to bring about an initial period of experimentation and innovation across a range of churches. In the 1970s this impulse waned in mainline congregations although it continued in many Pentecostal, nondenominational, and independent evangelical churches. Many of the megachurches that would later serve as testing and teaching churches got their start at that time or soon after in the 1980s. In the 1980s, too, the infrastructure for widespread dissemination of new worship music was developed. That decade also saw the last gasps of archaic English in Protestant worship. Elsewhere the theologians of the phenomenon, largely

---

30. By acknowledging these multiple points of origin and influences on contemporary worship's development we hope to make more complex the picture that has been drawn by liturgical historians. In our opinion these historians often have been too mesmerized by a single source and expression of contemporary worship, namely, the pragmatic strand seen in the church growth movement and in certain influential megachurches.

Pentecostal, were developing a theoretical undergirding. Thus the 1980s was a period of important incubation.

The 1990s exploded as a wide breadth of churches became aware of this alternative style of worship. Congregations wanting to explore adopting it had prominent churches to teach them how and had a burgeoning supply of published resources and music to facilitate new services. Widespread adoption of the term *contemporary worship* by the mid-1990s gave the phenomenon a name by which it could be branded, promoted, and embraced. The term also set up a binary contrast with traditional worship, which led to wars across congregations and denominations.

Since the late 1990s there have been additional developments in contemporary worship as the phenomenon has matured and diversified. A new generation of songwriters have updated and diversified the sound of the music. The technological sophistication of contemporary worship has jumped light-years since that time. Older hymns have been retuned and ancient liturgies have been rediscovered. What teachers and conferences considered cutting edge has changed even as the phenomenon's root sensibilities stay the same. And the phenomenon has come under closer academic scrutiny as a young generation of ethnomusicologists has focused on this phenomenon's music.

And the occasional liturgical scholar even has the audacity to think it is time to tell the history of contemporary worship, too! (Hint: the authors of this book.) We invite you to share our audacity and read on.

Chapter 2
TIME IN CONTEMPORARY WORSHIP

The liturgical issue of time is the center of contemporary worship, literally so. Temp, the root of *contemporary*, comes from the Latin word for *time, tempus*. In English several words are derived from that root, such as *extemporaneous, temporary, tempo,* and *temporal. Contemporary* is another. To be contemporary is to be with (*con-*) the time (*tempus*). As applied to worship, to be with the time (*con-tempus,* or *contemporary*) has meant not only to be of the time but to belong to the people of that time. In any of the surges of the use of the term *contemporary worship,* whether in the 1960s or the 1990s, that concern for fittingness was what was meant. Contemporary worship is the worship of a specific people's language. It is worship that played their music. It is worship that arose from their concerns and spoke to them. It is worship fitting to their world and thus owned by that people. Contemporary worship is worship that is with it, the "it" being a particular people's time.

While this stress on fittingness might not always have been at the forefront in the history of Christian worship generally, the concern with time has been. As liturgical historian James White has noted, time is a "language" through which Christians have expressed their worship.[1] How various Christians have organized and kept time speaks much about how they view themselves, their world, their worship, and, ultimately, about Christianity itself and the vision of God whom they worship. As time is not an incidental element in the salvation that God has accomplished—we call it salvation *history* for a reason—neither has it been a peripheral matter in various approaches to Christian worship. Organizing time has been an essential aspect of all forms of Christian worship.

And yet it is more. Because worship is dealing with a God who is not just of this world and its temporality, how time is organized and managed in worship has tended to be more than just a functional tool. Time has also had

---

1. James F. White, *Introduction to Christian Worship*, 3rd ed. (Nashville: Abingdon Press, 2000), 47.

a symbolic quality by which Christians believe they encounter an eternal God whose works have cosmic significance. It wasn't just for fun that Christians shifted the main day for worship from the Sabbath, the seventh day, to Sunday, the first day of the week. It was because they saw themselves in worship as somehow experiencing the Risen Lord on his day. That symbolic association with time is true for contemporary worshipper too, although how they think about time as a symbol mediating this encounter is new.

From one angle, contemporary worship's approach to liturgical time is not novel at all. It rides on the coattails of previous patterns of Christian worship, especially Protestant Free Church approaches. For example, Free Church worship has tended to have a simple yearly calendar when compared to the classic calendar that had developed by the Middle Ages and been found in Protestant liturgical traditions with a stronger propensity for inheriting ancient forms (e.g., Lutheran or Anglican/Episcopal) or reappropriating them (e.g., Methodist or Presbyterian). In other words, Christmas and Easter might be celebrated, but little else from ancient calendars. What was true of Baptists in 1710 and Pentecostals in 1910 is still true of Baptist and Pentecostal contemporary worshippers in 2010: compared to 1010, their yearly calendar is simple and straightforward.

But from another angle, contemporary worship's sense of time is novel. It sometimes has eroded the symbolic importance of Sunday itself. Even more important, contemporary worship has introduced a view of liturgical time exceptional in the history of Christian worship through extended sets of songs with seamless flow. In contemporary worship, these extended times of uninterrupted congregational singing is the time-related symbol to encounter God and participate in angelic, heavenly worship beyond time. Moreover, since the advent of new technology around the turn of the century, many churches are giving unprecedented focus to the management of time in a worship service, raising the significance of time in worship even higher.

And so let's consider the *temp* of con*temp*orary worship. It's time.

CONTEMPORARY WORSHIP AND CLASSIC RHYTHMS OF TIME

Most classic primers on Christian worship give an overview of the classic rhythms of liturgical time for the day, the week, and the year.[2] The day

---

2. See Laurence Hull Stookey, *Calendar: Christ's Time for the Church* (Nashville: Abingdon Press, 1996) or chapter 2 in White, *Introduction to Christian Worship* as examples.

consists of multiple times of prayer, with prayer services (called a daily *office* in the West) in the morning and evening especially important and common. The week centers on Sunday, the first day of the week, the day of Christ's resurrection. Worshipping on Sunday is a living commemoration of that climatic saving act of God in Christ. The year expands the commemoration of God's activity in Christ through seasons of preparation and celebration. Preparing for Christ's coming (both first and second) during Advent gives way to the joyous celebration of his birth at Christmas and revealing to the world at Epiphany. In the same way, Lent's focused attention on the cross and faith climaxes in the day-by-day commemorations of Christ's ministry during Holy Week. Those commemorations themselves are eclipsed by the boundless joy of the resurrection at Easter, a celebration that continues unabated for fifty days through the remembrance of God's outpouring of the Holy Spirit at Pentecost. Churches more attentive to the year might include other feasts like those that commemorate other events in the life of Christ (his baptism, his circumcision, his presentation in the temple, or his Ascension, for example) or others that remember additional aspects to the divine economy like God's Triune nature (Trinity Sunday). Roman Catholic and Eastern Christians would also consider the sanctoral cycle, the yearly commemoration of saints.

Whether the daily, weekly, or yearly rhythms, this shaping of time was hammered out over the first centuries of church history and remained stable thereafter. The status of these classic rhythms has fluctuated in Protestant worship history, however. Different Protestants in diverse eras have followed these rhythms to varying extents. By the mid-twentieth century, American Protestants of all sorts paid less attention to daily rhythms outside encouraging individual times of prayer and Bible reading. The weekly rhythm focused on Sunday with a late morning time standard. Many congregations had additional services for the same worshippers on Sunday evening and Wednesday night. Some of these churches emphasized evangelistic goals in their Sunday evening services. Congregations differed in approach to the year, too. Liturgically conservative traditions like Lutherans or Episcopalians had a fuller schedule of yearly feasts and seasons. On the other end of the spectrum, Free Church congregations might celebrate only Christmas and Easter along with other occasions like the yearly revival, Mission Sunday, or civic holidays.

With respect to daily rhythms, there has been no change at all since there was nothing really to change. But that is not the case with weekly and yearly rhythms. The rise of contemporary worship has meant a dramatic shift in weekly rhythms and slightly less so in yearly ones.

Contemporary worship's approach to weekly rhythms of time has been shaped by pragmatic thinking, by maintaining prior practices, or by both in some congregations. Which of these factors has been the most important has depended upon which model a congregation used to implement contemporary worship. Those churches intentionally adding a stylistically different service were pragmatic when deciding when to schedule the new service. Many pastors also had to consider the political dynamics within their congregations in scheduling the new service. These concerns were especially true for mainline congregations. On the other hand, churches that transformed existing service(s) into a contemporary style continued prior practices unless numeric growth made adding more services necessary.

Models for Implementing Contemporary Worship

- A new church start in which contemporary worship is indigenous to the people and unplanned

- A new church start in which contemporary worship is a predetermined, tactical decision

- Adding a new contemporary service within an existing congregation

- Morphing a congregation's already established service out of several services within that congregation

- Transitioning a congregation's single service without major alterations to the congregation's overall life

- Complete metamorphosis of a congregation involving worship as well as the nature of church life itself (e.g., location, building, organization, leadership, name)

In the pragmatic assessment of time the approach to the week was shaped by discerning what was convenient for people, especially if a new service was being targeted toward a particular group. The result in many instances was a proliferation of services within a congregation, each with its own targeted group, with varying degrees of attachment to Sunday.

The push for multiplying services was strong since the 1980s, especially from church growth experts, even before the specific promotion of contemporary services to mainline congregations. A standard rule of thumb offered to incite a desire to add a service was the 80 percent rule: if your worship space was 80 percent full, it was time to start a new service. The promise of success was enticing. One popular author, for instance, noted that four out of five congregations that moved from one service to two saw an increase in attendance.[3] Foremost when considering when to time a new service was assessing the life rhythms of those one hoped to attract, not any symbolic meaning to Sunday. Thus worship on Saturday evenings was promoted as a good possibility if a church wanted to reach those who had to work on Sundays or who wanted to preserve Sunday as family or recreation time.

When the term *contemporary worship* surged in the 1990s, these pragmatic voices soon added a specific appeal that new services ought to be in this new style. Thus mainline congregations began associating starting a new service generally with starting a contemporary service specifically.

Some tried the approach of the influential megachurch in Illinois, Willow Creek Community Church, when adding a contemporary service, which was to draw a clear distinction between seeker- and believer-oriented services. At Willow Creek, the (contemporary) seeker services were on Saturdays and Sundays and the believer services were mid-week.[4]

A more common approach has been the multiplying of services differentiated by style, not by seeker and believer targeting. In innumerable congregations the labels *contemporary* and *traditional* became the way to set up a clear binary between two stylistic options in worship.[5] The challenges in those instances were contests about the best time for the contemporary service or introducing the congregation to a more contemporary style itself. Leaders used a range of time-related tactics. Some used special occasions like "Youth Sundays" to acclimate their congregation to something different. Another way to introduce contemporary worship into a congregation was to use a mid-week service that was less attended. That's what Faithful Central Baptist

---

3. Lyle E. Schaller, *44 Ways to Increase Church Attendance* (Nashville: Abingdon Press, 1988), 49–50.

4. For more details of that decade's practices, see Lester Ruth, "*Lex Agendi, Lex Orandi*: Toward an Understanding of Seeker Services as a New Kind of Liturgy," *Worship* 70, no. 5 (September 1996): 386–405.

5. The work of ethnomusicologist Deborah R. Justice is insightful on this issue. See, for example, "The Curious Longevity of the Traditional-Contemporary Divide: Mainline Musical Choices in Post-Worship War America," *Liturgy* 32, no. 1 (2017): 16–23.

Church in Inglewood, California, did in 1988.[6] Others sought times that those opposed to contemporary worship found more tolerable because the times weren't considered "real" worship times. Such times could include a Saturday night service for nearby college students or a service held during the Sunday School hour. Such options could seem less threatening to those who didn't want a new, contemporary service competing with their much-loved traditional one.

Once introduced, the timing for a contemporary service could continue to evolve. Some churches discovered their contemporary service had outgrown the traditional in attendance. If so, the time for the services might be flip-flopped so the contemporary had a more desirable time slot. Sometimes two traditional services were consolidated and moved to an earlier time on Sunday to free up the "prime time" for the contemporary service. And other congregations found that targeting mattered little. People came to whatever service was most convenient for themselves or their families.

New church plants in which contemporary worship was the only style, or congregations that had a complete metamorphosis, tended to offer services according to previous schedules or at times based on availability of staff and appeal to worshippers. Larger congregations often moved to multiple services on Sunday morning or other times on the weekend such as Saturday evening.

With respect to the Christian year, a concern with being relevant to worshippers is a factor that has kept in check a fuller following of the year (not to mention Free Church leaders' unfamiliarity with it). This concern with relevance is tied to a strategic concern for evangelistic success. In this perspective, the language of Christian time erodes the ability to do effective outreach to the unchurched. By creating its own distinctive world (including the world of time), the church is in danger of being ineffective with unchurched people because they cannot easily break into that world.[7]

The result is a kind of hybrid year, drawing upon a few feasts or seasons when they already are in sync with cultural rhythms. However, instead of using these feasts or seasons as the centerpiece for a full classic year, they are combined with a series of scripture readings and sermons that are fitting

---

6. Birgitta J. Johnson, "'This Is Not the Warm-Up Act!': How Praise and Worship Reflects Expanding Musical Traditions and Theology in a Bapticostal Charismatic African American Megachurch" in *The Spirit of Praise: Music and Worship in Global Pentecostal-Charismatic Christianity*, ed. Monique M. Ingalls and Amos Yong (University Park: The Pennsylvania State University Press, 2015), 121.

7. For an example, see Nelson Searcy and Jason Hatley, *Engage: A Guide to Creating Life-Transforming Worship Services* (Grand Rapids: Baker Books, 2011), 66–67.

to culturally formed rhythms and expectations of worshippers, that is, the "real calendar" or "the normal year that shapes the lives of ordinary people" as one creator of an alternative lectionary put it.[8] Since large numbers of visitors come on Christmas and Easter, for example, this approach could focus the content of worship on evangelistic series in the weeks after each of those feasts.[9]

A disregard with the classic year has not been the only approach within contemporary worship. There has been a yearly calendar creep among some Free Church Protestants, whether Pentecostal or just evangelical, as in tweaking weeks of Christmas preparation into a season of Advent. The attraction to the classic yearly seasons and feasts seems strongest when there is a particular symbol that proves appealing (e.g., an Advent wreath) or the commemoration focuses on a critical part of the biblical story of salvation (e.g., Christ's death).

An attachment to the classic year seems stronger for mainline congregations but extends beyond too. For example, *Worship Times: A Newsletter for the Creative Worship Leader*, the publication that preceded *Worship Leader* magazine, dedicated an entire issue (Fall 1988) to teaching about Advent. And Pentecostal author LaMar Boschman spent a whole chapter in his 1994 book laying out the shape of the year.[10] Both examples showed the influence of Robert Webber, a well-known author and speaker at that time, who popularized ancient features of worship like the calendar within his larger emphasis on drawing upon early Christian sources to renew worship today.

Overall, implementing a fuller church year has been sporadic in contemporary worship. For some early adopters the obstacle was a lack of appropriate music fitting a contemporary style. One author noted, for example, the anomaly that Christmas created in many congregations: "many churches seem to abandon their distinctive praise-and-worship format for conventional Christmas carols, resulting in a disconcerting shift in the ambiance and thrust of worship."[11]

---

8. Thomas G. Bandy, *Introducing the Uncommon Lectionary: Opening the Bible to Seekers and Disciples* (Nashville: Abingdon Press, 2006), 46.

9. See Searcy and Hatley, *Engage,* and Adam Hamilton, *Unleashing the Word: Preaching with Relevance, Purpose, and Passion* (Nashville: Abingdon Press, 2003).

10. LaMar Boschman, *A Heart of Worship: Experience a Rebirth of Worship* (Lake Mary, FL: Creation House, 1994).

11. Randolph W. Sly, "Charismatic Churches," in *The Services of the Christian Year*, vol. 5 of *The Complete Library of Christian Worship*, ed. Robert E. Webber (Nashville: StarSong, 1994), 15. Other articles in this volume give signs about the varying levels of adoption of the year.

FLOW AS THE CONSTRUCTION OF TIME

Regardless of what contemporary churches have done with weekly and yearly rhythms of time, managing time within a service has been the key temporal aspect. And the central concern of this ordering and managing has been in achieving flow, understood as the smooth sequencing of elements of a service, especially the songs within a worship set.

Flow as strived for in contemporary worship is a time issue in several respects. For one thing, sequencing is about deciding what act of worship comes before another in time. Secondly, the desire for good flow involves avoiding periods of unnecessary "dead time" in worship, that is, when nothing purposeful is happening. For many, to have dead time is the kiss of death in worship. Finally, flow is a time issue because those who instruct about how to achieve flow teach attentiveness to the tempo and pace of acts of worship, especially the songs. They do so to enable a ubiquitous aim expressed throughout the history of contemporary worship: flow should facilitate worshippers having an experience with God. As experienced Vineyard worship leader Carl Tuttle expressed it in 1987, "Grouping songs in such a way that they flow together and make sense is essential to a good worship experience."[12] A Pentecostal contemporary to Tuttle stated the same understanding in a more theological way: the goal of the worship leader in planning and leading a flowing worship set "is to bring the congregational worshippers into a corporate awareness of God's manifest Presence."[13]

The concern for flow in extended times of congregational singing has been a constant since at least the 1970s. The concern first arose in Pentecostal strands of contemporary worship as teachings about praise, worship, and God's presence (see chapters 7 and 8 for more history) became associated with extended times of congregational singing, soon to be known as worship or praise sets of songs. That Pentecostals would emphasize flow was natural since it was an idea connected to how they saw the Holy Spirit operating in an anointed service. And the inherent experiential aspects of flow—it is

---

12. Carl Tuttle, "Song Selection & New Song Introduction," in *Worship Leaders Training Manual* (Anaheim, CA: Worship Resource Center/Vineyard Ministries International, 1987), 141. In this essay, Tuttle gave thirty examples of song sets that had good flow.

13. Barry Griffing, "Releasing Charismatic Worship," in *Restoring Praise & Worship to the Church*, ed. David Blomgren, Dean Smith, and Douglas Christoffel (Shippensburg, PA: Revival Press, 1989), 92.

perceived experientially and it contributes to having positive experiences—fit with classic Pentecostal emphases on experience in worship.

By 1978 Pentecostals were publishing guides on how to achieve flow in a song set. David Blomgren's is perhaps the earliest.[14] In a section on how to use scripture choruses, Blomgren laid out an approach to flow whose central features has remained constant since then. He portrayed three ambitions in having flow in the worship set: the flow should move continuously with no interruptions; the flow should move naturally (using connections from the songs' content, keys, and tempos); and the flow should move toward a goal of a climatic experience of true worship of God. Blomgren spelled out technical aspects for achieving proper flow: the content of the songs in sequence makes sense, having scriptural and thematic relatedness; the key signatures are conducive to easy, unjarring, and smooth transitions between songs; the tempo of the songs (usually faster to slower overall with songs having similar tempos grouped) contributing to a growing sense of closer encounter with God; and talking is used sparingly, pointedly, and purposefully. To help plan and lead, Blomgren encouraged worship leaders to have a master list of songs with their critical elements identified to be used in planning and as a handy reference for when the Spirit might call for spontaneous changes in a service.

The essentials of Blomgren's approach have remained steady through four decades of guides on achieving flow in a worship set. That constancy does not reflect Blomgren's specific influence as much as it shows how widespread the desire and standard techniques for flow have become.

By the mid-1980s several theoretical models existed to guide sequencing songs to achieve flow. Vineyard worship leader Eddie Espinosa (whose prior experience was in a California Pentecostal church, Faith Assembly Revival Fellowship, in the late 1960s and early 1970s) provided a summary of four such models in 1987.[15] Two were based on Psalms: the Psalm 95 model and the Psalm 100 model. The Psalm 95 approach first used rejoicing songs, then thanking, praising, and finally reverencing songs. The Psalm 100 model, according to Espinosa, was a journey into the holy of holies of the temple or tabernacle. It first involved encampment outside the structure through "fun songs," then songs of gratitude, followed by worship songs as worshippers entered the holy place, and finally intimate songs of God's presence in the holy of holies. The mood of the songs in these two models shifts from being more upbeat to more reflective. Another model is based on the use of the songs: the

---

14.   David K. Blomgren, *The Song of the Lord* (Portland: Bible Press, 1978), 29–31.

15.   Eddie Espinosa, "Worship Leading," in *Worship Leaders Training Manual* (Anaheim, CA: Worship Resource Center/Vineyard Ministries International, 1987), 81–82.

flow should go from singing about God, to singing to each other (that is, in encouragement or exhortation), to singing to God. Finally, Espinosa spelled out a relationship approach to constructing a worship set for flow. The terms for the different phases reflect different ways of relating between God and a worshipper. Starting with an invitation or call to worship, the songs moved to an initial engagement with, then exaltation in glorifying God, followed by love songs directly adoring God, and finally to intimacy with God. Although Espinosa did not list it as the Vineyard model, it was usually associated with this movement.

Although Espinosa's summary is not exhaustive, it outlines some of the most common models that circulated. What was common to all explanations was a sense of musical journey into the presence of God. The journey motif became a common description of what worship leaders sought to achieve by flow. Examples from the period across different racial expressions of contemporary worship show similar sense of movement. Thus the 1980 sets from Espinosa's white Anaheim Vineyard congregation show resemblance with the sets from the black West Angeles Church of God in Christ.[16]

No single model for explaining flow ever won out across contemporary worship even though the musical techniques for achieving flow stayed the same. Indeed, some resisted the notion that there was anything as *the* model. And as the explanations for flow spread from their Pentecostal roots and became more widespread, their theoretical descriptions morphed.

Saddleback, a megachurch in California, is a case in point. In 1985 a young musician, Rick Muchow, was touring with his music group and happened to go to a Hope Chapel in Hermosa Beach. There he learned something new: flow in a set as journey into the holy of holies.[17] Muchow took this new insight with him when hired in 1987 to do music at Saddleback Community Church. There Muchow and pastor Rick Warren transformed the explanation for flow without changing its intent or the method for achieving. Their desire was an approach to worship that was seeker sensitive and purposefully evangelistic. The result was an acronym, IMPACT, which they used to guide that church's approach to ordering a service. The sequence in flow was to move from songs that <u>i</u>nspire <u>m</u>ovement to <u>p</u>raise to <u>a</u>doration to <u>c</u>ommitment to

---

16. We have listened to worship in 1982 from the Anaheim congregation on a privately made cassette tape. The COGIC material can be found on a CD by the West Angeles Church of God in Christ Mass Choir and Congregation entitled *Saints in Praise*, vol. 1, directed by Patrick Henderson, recorded March 23, 1989 (The Sparrow Corporation, 1989), compact disc.

17. Rick Muchow, interview by Lester Ruth, March 9, 2015.

a song to tie it together.[18] As a working model this acronym was sometimes expressed by a short-cut that focused on worshippers' involvement and the mood: the songs should move from a "hand clapper" (an up-beat song about God) to a "hand holder" (a community song where the worshipping assembly engages as one in dialogue with God), to a "hand raiser" (a more intimate song where the worshipper sings in the first person to God), and then, at the end of the service, another "hand holder."[19] Warren advocated the IMPACT model for flow in his hugely popular books as well as in his conference speaking, as did Muchow. Warren combined the model with observations about the general necessity to speed up worship music in churches as well as using music to set the appropriate mood for worship.[20]

From Warren's writings and Saddleback's conferences, at which both Warren and Muchow would teach, others picked up this morphed sense of flow, adapted it further, and applied it to their own context. One example is Timothy Wright, who in the 1980s and 1990s was the associate pastor at Community Church of Joy in Phoenix, Arizona. This Lutheran congregation became a cutting-edge congregation for promoting contemporary worship within mainline circles. (Wright's book, *A Community of Joy: How to Create Contemporary Worship*, was an early how-to guide in the 1990s to use the term *contemporary worship* in the title.) Wright picked up his sense of flow and mood from hearing Warren speak on energy levels for a whole service.[21]

Even though the ways in which Warren and Wright spoke about flow in worship differed from the earlier, "classic" Pentecostal articulations of the same, they all shared the necessity to have good flow and understanding how it was achieved. There was also a basic sense of what flow ought to be. The justification given for flow was where they differed significantly. The overt theological and biblical explanations earlier Pentecostals used gave way to more general explanations by evangelical and mainline proponents about worshippers having a positive experience of God and of the service.

Aiming for good flow in a worship set soon extended to a desire for seamless flow for an entire service. Authors from a variety of viewpoints began advocating a concern for whole service flow by the late 1980s and throughout the 1990s. Church growth expert Lyle Schaller, for example, argued that all

---

18.   Rick Muchow, e-mail to Lester Ruth, May 9, 2015.

19.   Rick Muchow, interview by Swee Hong Lim and Lester Ruth, April 30, 2015.

20.   Rick Warren, *The Purpose Driven Church: Growth without Compromising Your Message & Mission* (Grand Rapids: Zondervan Publishing House, 1995), 256, 286–87.

21.   Timothy Wright, interview by Lester Ruth, February 6, 2015.

churches ought to pick up the pace of their services and avoid "dead spots" because slow pace and dead time bore people. And bored worshippers do not come to church.[22] The overriding question for Schaller and others who advocated whole service flow was an experiential one: would contemporary worshippers find the service to be a positive, pleasing experience? By the late 1990s the result in many churches was an approach to a group-based, worship planning process that sought to make the entire service seamless and coherent with respect to its content and acts of worship. As one such worship designer put it, the goal was a service where the right act of worship was in the right spot at the right time, with a context established for why it is present, with no dead spots before or after. The key was integration along with smooth segues, thus requiring those leading worship to be in the right spot at the right time, too.[23] In other words, some of the same techniques developed for creating flow within music sets have been applied to the service as a whole.

TENSIONS IN TIME IN CONTEMPORARY WORSHIP

A great irony in the history of contemporary worship is that many of its roots are in liturgical traditions that value extemporaneity in worship although its development is toward closer management of time. From being an extemporaneous phenomenon (ex-temp = out of time, beyond time) contemporary worship in many congregations has become *intemporaneous* (bound to time, in-time), to coin a new word.

Part of this closer management of time in a service can be attributed to churches valuing tight, whole service flow. When this level of flow was a goal, worship planners brought over production values from outside the church—like forms of entertainment—to give a sense of what good flow felt like. Some advocated close timing of each act of worship when planning and careful construction of the transitions to achieve a higher level of professionalism in the service.[24] For others, even precise timing for transitions was crucial. Thus various authors have advocated a "five-second rule," that is, do not allow for more than five seconds where nothing is happening (the dreaded "dead

22. Schaller, *44 Ways to Increase Church Attendance*, 32–33.

23. Kim Miller, *[Re]Designing Worship: Creating Powerful God Experiences* (Nashville: Abingdon Press, 2009), 99.

24. Lynn Hurst, *Changing Your Tune! The Musician's Handbook for Creating Contemporary Worship* (Nashville: Abingdon Press, 1999), 77.

spot.") Some influential churches implemented this high level of production values early. For instance, tapes of Willow Creek Community Church from the early 1990s show seamless, quick flow through the whole service.[25]

The intemporaneity of contemporary worship has developed hand in hand with the increasing sophistication of technology in worship. Early forms of contemporary worship with simpler technology could enable worship in ways much more open-ended and free flowing with respect to time. Acoustic instruments freed musicians from a sound board. Master lists of the congregation's entire song repertoire allowed the worship leader to extend or contract the worship set as seemed appropriate. (Remember that these lists had songs divided by key, tempo, and theme.) Worshippers accessed song lyrics either from memory, from mimeographed booklets, or perhaps even a hymnal. Eventually overhead projectors became popular but, even then, switching out transparencies could happen quickly. (Shorter lyrics in the average song made things simpler, too.) Thus Carl Tuttle could lead for his 1982 Anaheim Vineyard congregation a seamless worship set lasting almost fifty minutes, consisting of sixteen different songs, with no preplanning and no presentation of lyrics to the congregation whatsoever.[26]

The advent of more sophisticated ways of providing lyrics to the songs was a significant step toward more precise management of liturgical time in contemporary worship. The move to slides to project the lyrics was one such advancement. The slides had to be placed in a predetermined order in their carousel. Once projection began, it was much easier to continue this order in sequence than it was to do things extemporaneously. By the mid- to late 1990s many churches had taken another step by utilizing computer projection to present song lyrics. Although sophisticated software like ProPresenter and MediaShout allows immediate access to lyrics of any song in a digital library, a common practice is to go with what has been preselected.

With better projectors, computers, screens, and in-house cameras came the ability to coordinate with other media elements, like video clips, motion backgrounds, live shots of worship leaders or pastors, and, recently, environmental projection. Significant advances in these elements began around the turn of the century and have increased significantly within the last few years. Each technological advancement nudged congregations toward a closer management of time. More technological moving parts required closer

---

25. *An Inside Look at the Willow Creek Seeker Service: Show Me the Way* (Grand Rapids: Zondervan, 1992), videocassette (VHS); *An Inside Look at the Willow Creek Worship Service: Building a New Community* (Grand Rapids: Zondervan, 1992), videocassette (VHS).

26. Our observations are based on an unpublished audio tape of a 1982 service.

coordination to provide seamless flow in the service. And closer coordination necessitated tighter management of time. As the technological bar rose so did the impulse toward intemporaneity.

The increasing levels of technology allow the average worship to perceive spontaneity and extemporaneity that are not actually there.[27] In-ear monitors for musicians allow them to receive direction from the technology staff and well as follow click tracks that set a firm, predetermined tempo for songs. Music tracks add instrumental sounds to the sound heard by worshipper but require preset tempos for songs too. Back monitors permit the technology staff to communicate messages to the stage and show musicians and preachers countdown clocks to the next item in the order of worship. Headphones with microphones let technology staff in the worship space (e.g., with the sound mixing board) and in remote centers like video control booths talk to each other, call out countdowns to the next act of worship, direct camera operators, and make sure that whatever is projected is the correct item. Active chat windows on computer screens give intemporaneity across space as remote campuses coordinate with streaming from the home church. And so, in these dimensions and others beyond the perception of the average worship, there can be a tight management of time in a technologically advanced contemporary service.

The growing management of time—the tendency for contemporaneous worship to move from being extemporaneous to intemporaneous—has produced tension in some of the churches that originated and adopted contemporary worship. That tension arose when a liturgical tradition saw extemporaneity as a mark of worship that is true and of the Holy Spirit, that is, worship in Spirit and in truth (John 4:24). This view of extemporaneity has been held widely within Free Church ways of worship. Pentecostals especially have valued extemporaneity, spontaneity, and flexibility as essential for being able to respond to the Spirit's leading in worship.

By the late 1980s, as a sense of what a worship set looked like became more commonplace, their literature on contemporary worship felt a need to address the tension. Barry Griffing, for example, called out "Pentecostal traditionalism" that overstated spontaneity as the only way for worship to be of the Spirit. Griffing was concerned that Pentecostal worship leaders would not consider preparing beforehand their "sacrifices of praise" in an order of worship. Using the example of David in 1 Chronicles, he argued that preparation need not hinder responding to the Spirit of God in worship but could

---

27. Will Doggett, interview by Lester Ruth, July 17, 2014.

release it.[28] What was needed was both a plan and the worship leader's active discernment of the Spirit's guiding. Thus in 1995 one author noted the range of acceptable options to live in the tension: prepare a song list for the worship set, don't prepare a list, or prepare a list but follow the Lord's leading "to do different songs during the actual service."[29]

Since then, the tension has lessened as regular patterns for contemporary worship have emerged and technological advances have required greater time coordination within a service. That lessening seems true across a range of churches, whether Free Church or mainline (which traditionally have been more willing to live with preplanning).

---

28.   Griffing, "Releasing Charismatic Worship," 94–95.

29.   Scott Brenner, "Song Selection for Worship Leaders" in *Let Your Glory Fall: Songs & Essays* (Anaheim, CA: Vineyard Music Group, 1995), 270.

Chapter 3
THE SPACE OF CONTEMPORARY WORSHIP

In telling any history it is easy for the eye to wander to dramatic examples. That focusing has happened in some previous accounts of contemporary worship as some authors focused on a few megachurches to tell this story. That tendency has shaped the best books on the architectural dimensions of contemporary worship, too. These books, looking at the largest churches, portray the history of contemporary worship space as a journey from point A to point B: from meetinghouse to megachurch, for example, or from church to theater.[1] Such depictions are accurate in as much as they document a few megachurches intentionally constructed for contemporary worship.

To tell a fuller history of the spaces used for contemporary worship, however, we should look beyond large congregations. A more complete story of contemporary worship space would need to look at a range of churches of various types and sizes, and how they changed many different kinds of previous spaces. The resulting history should note the amazing range of transitions that have occurred: from fellowship hall to sanctuary, from Family Life Center or multipurpose room to worship center, or from theater or office complex to worship space. The history for other congregations would be a tale of how they renovated (or did not renovate) their former sanctuary, built for one style of worship, to handle a more contemporary style. From this approach, the story is as much about adapting as it is about designing new spaces.

Moreover, a fuller history of contemporary worship spaces must take into account the impact that ever cheaper—yet more sophisticated—technology has had on contemporary worship. The effect of technological advancements

---

1. Anne C. Loveland and Otis B. Wheeler, *From Meetinghouse to Megachurch: A Material and Cultural History* (Columbia: University of Missouri Press, 2003); Jeanne Halgren Kilde, *When Church Became Theatre: The Transformation of Evangelical Architecture and Worship in Nineteenth-Century America* (New York: Oxford University Press, 2002).

has brought about spatial dimensions exceptional in the history of Christian worship. For example, technology enables moving from a single-dimensional space in which everyone sees and hears the same thing to multidimensional spaces in which worshippers experience one world of sound, musicians another, and the technology staff still another. In addition, the advancement of digital technologies and the capacity for streaming now means that a worshipping congregation can be spread across multiple spaces on a single campus or even across multiple campuses.

We will proceed in this chapter by taking a look at larger developments at both the general architecture of contemporary worship and significant technological developments. We will conclude by comparing typical contemporary worship spaces, especially as the form has developed within the last several years, to classic features of Christian liturgical architecture.

HISTORICAL DEVELOPMENTS IN CONTEMPORARY WORSHIP SPACE

The history of space in contemporary worship is not a straightforward journey. It is reasonable to say that congregations have used several approaches to find a space for contemporary services. Some have appropriated an existing space and simply inserted a contemporary service into it, making only minimal, impermanent changes. This minimalist approach applies to spaces both originally intended for worship and those that were not. Other congregations have adapted an existing space, making significant changes to it to accommodate contemporary worship. Again that applies to all kinds of prior spaces. Some congregations aimed for a blurry midpoint between these first two options by perhaps making one significant change but leaving the rest of the space unaffected permanently. Finally, others have specifically designed a space for contemporary worship, taking their sense of what's required for contemporary worship and shaping a space to match this vision.

The main approach to finding a space for contemporary worship has shifted over time. Through the 1980s, venues for contemporary worship were overwhelmingly appropriated or adapted spaces. The most straightforward approach was simple occupation of a space and conducting a contemporary service in it without physical modifications. That applies not only to services for hippies in the Jesus People movement in the early 1970s but also to mainline liturgical experiments in youth rooms, church camps, charismatic retreat centers, and prayer chapels. If a congregation was small and the musical instrument was an acoustic guitar, a congregation could simply occupy almost any space and hold a contemporary service. At the initial services for Hope Chapel Windward Oahu in Hawaii, for example, worshippers sat on the ground or in lawn chairs at an oceanfront park.[2]

Some early adaptations involved fairly minimal changes to the space. Even for cutting-edge congregations it wasn't a particular kind of space that was needed but other liturgical features. In the late 1970s John Wimber, soon to be instrumental as the national leader of Vineyard churches, noted these features could be quite minimal. Preaching in his humorous, tongue-in-cheek manner, Wimber told his Anaheim, California, congregation around the start of 1979 that what was needed for a new, successful contemporary church plant in southern California was a short list: "a Bible, a teacher, and a rock band."[3] Seemingly whatever space could accommodate these elements could be adapted for contemporary worship. Wimber's own congregation was a case in point, traveling a long sojourn of appropriation and adaptation as it grew rapidly in its first years: beginning as a home group in 1976, it publicly launched in a Mason Lodge in 1997, utilized various school gyms, and then moved to a warehouse in 1983.[4] Finally, in the early 1990s, it moved into the former Rockwell International Testing Laboratory in Anaheim, California, adapting it for contemporary worship.

Not all adaptations were as massive, however. At Chicago's Ravenswood Evangelical Covenant Church in the late 1980s and early 1990s, for example, there was no massive overhaul of its sanctuary as the congregation made its worship more contemporary. The band was placed at pew level in an available spot at the front and the pulpit was removed.[5] Between Anaheim Vineyard's large renovation and Ravenswood's small one, there are countless variations on the theme of adapting church and secular spaces for contemporary worship. Among the more common spaces to be adapted are fellowship halls, youth rooms, and family life centers/multipurpose rooms among church-related spaces. Occasionally a sense of irony characterizes an adaptation. Dallas's First Baptist Church, for example, changed the platform in its historic 1892 sanctuary—what's more traditional than a nineteenth-century

---

2. Ralph Moore, *Let Go of the Ring* (Honolulu: Straight Street Publishing, 1983), 133.

3. John Wimber, "Don't Lose Your First Love" in *The Ministry and Teaching of John Wimber* series, CD#310 (Doin' the Stuff/Vineyard Music Group, 2004).

4. See Andy Park, Lester Ruth, and Cindy Rethmeier, *Worshiping with the Anaheim Vineyard: The Emergence of Contemporary Worship* (Grand Rapids: Wm. B. Eerdmans Publishing Co., 2017).

5. James F. Caccamo, Todd E. Johnson, and Lester Ruth, *Living Worship: A Multimedia Resource for Students and Leaders,* DVD (Grand Rapids: Brazos Press, 2010).

sanctuary?—to make it a home for a contemporary service.[6] Congregations have adapted, too, a range of nonchurch facilities including coffeehouses, school gyms and auditoriums, office complexes, and warehouses.

As a distinct sense of contemporary worship service has developed, more churches have begun to design spaces for it. Perhaps Willow Creek Community Church was among the first, completing its auditorium in 1981.[7] (Prior to that it used a movie theater.) Carpenter's Home Church in Lakeland, Florida, was another congregation specifically designing a space. In 1985 it built a space incorporating two large, built-in screens for IMAG (image magnification from camera shots) of its preachers.[8]

Specific design for contemporary worship accelerated in the 1990s. In this decade a clearer sense of what a contemporary service required came into focus. Contemporary worship gained a sense of having an identifiable form. Once congregations could envision what was entailed in a contemporary service they could begin to think about the best home for it. In addition, the growing prominence of several "contemporary" megachurches provided a model for contemporary worship. Attending a megachurch conference offered church leaders from around the nation a chance to become familiar with this way of worship and the type of space that housed it. Finally, in the latter half of the 1990s, technology crossed a threshold in terms of affordability. Average churches could set aside their older portable overhead projectors and contemplate where to place permanent screens, projectors, and the computers to run them. Building a specially designed building helped answer these technology-related questions.

Even though we have unfolded the three approaches—appropriation, adaptation, and intentional design—in sequential fashion, it would be a mistake to see these three approaches in a strict chronological manner. Although the early decades emphasized the first two approaches, there are still congregations that use appropriation and adaptation to find a home for their contemporary services. None of the three approaches has gone away.

Notwithstanding which approach has been used, certain qualities have tended to show up in spaces for contemporary worship. Perhaps the most striking and pervasive has been the centrality of musicians—vocalists and instrumentalists alike—in the space. Contemporary worshippers are used to

---

6. Jerry Halcomb, interview by Lester Ruth, September 27, 2016.

7. Loveland and Wheeler, *From Meetinghouse to Megachurch*, 122.

8. Ibid., 229–30.

seeing their musicians as they lead front, center, and usually elevated in the space. The recent use of IMAG reinforces their spatial centrality.

There's been a common reenvisioning of the spatial placement of the preacher as well. Gone is the spatial centrality of the preacher during a service, parked in a prominent, elevated chair at the front. Emphasis has been placed on the physical body of the preacher when speaking and less importance on a substantial pulpit. Even in the early 1970s liturgical historian James White had begun to call in question the propriety of prominent pulpits in light of a changed "social reality."[9] Some strands of contemporary worship still might incorporate a pulpit but many do not. Even if they do, IMAG allows listeners to see a preacher's facial expressions.

Another recurring quality has been reliance upon electronic technology. Even in the initial surge of contemporary worship in the late 1960s, advocates were calling for the use of better sound systems, film and slide projectors, and theatrical lighting. Indeed, by the mid-1980s, some complained that contemporary worship was too reliant: "many congregations are so dependent on modern technology—on the microphone, backup singers, and a pop-style band all organized by the worship leader—that they would find worship practically lifeless if the electric plug were pulled on the sound system."[10] The spatial provision for technology has only increased, especially since the late 1990s.

A final quality in contemporary worship spaces has been the expressive and relaxed ways worshippers conduct themselves in the space. There is a higher degree of physical expressiveness, especially for mainline contemporary worshippers. Contemporary worship has put the raising of hands on the map. Informality in worship has grown alongside the increased expressive. Consequently snacking on coffee and finger foods has also become commonplace in many services. More noticeably, worshippers in contemporary services tend to dress informally, reflecting a larger cultural shift toward dressing down. Such a trend began early in contemporary worship's history. The ability to come straight from beach to church was a feature that attracted hippies to Chuck Smith Sr.'s Calvary Chapel in Costa Mesa, California, in the early 1970s. But this shift in space-specific behavior was neither immediate nor universal. The cover of Pentecostal Bob Sorge's 1987 book on contemporary

---

9. James F. White, *New Forms of Worship* (Nashville: Abingdon Press, 1971), 182.

10. Paul Wohlgemuth, "Worshiping Worship or Worshiping God," *Worship Times: The Newsletter for the Creative Worship Leader* 2, no. 3 (Fall 1987): 5. The author was professor of music at Oral Roberts University.

worship still showed musicians in formal "Sunday clothes," as did the photographs in a 1991 issue of *Reformed Worship* on praise and worship.[11]

TECHNOLOGICAL ADVANCEMENTS IN CONTEMPORARY WORSHIP

Contemporary worship is imaginably the most electronically dependent form of worship in church history. Perhaps that's not saying much considering how plugged-in all modern life tends to be. But, nonetheless, this level of liturgical dependency is still striking in the 2,000 year history of Christian worship. Since the late 1990s the reliance upon electronic technology has grown exponentially. This growth has changed the character of contemporary worship, making technological needs and opportunities a critical consideration in the space for contemporary worship. "Where will we put the screen?"—*the* conundrum of the mid-1990s—is no longer the main question a congregation will address.[12]

The emergence of trade magazines, conferences, consultants, and church staff are good signs that something has reached a tipping point. For worship technology that time is the 1990s. Two important magazines launched in that decade: *Technologies for Worship* magazine in 1992 and *Church Production* in 1999.[13] Both publications were filled with articles discussing and advertisements offering technology aimed for liturgical use. Worship technology conferences began in the same decade, the Inspiration Technology Conferences sponsored by *Technologies for Worship* magazine being one of the first in 1993.[14] By 1999 this conference had one hundred twenty-three sessions considering "the best use of technology in worship." The sessions were divided

---

11. Bob Sorge, *Exploring Worship: A Practical Guide to Praise and Worship* (Canandaigua: Bob Sorge, 1987); *Reformed Worship* 20 (June 1991).

12. Despite the importance of technology in contemporary worship, the topic is understudied by scholars. There are two important dissertations: Eileen Crowley-Horak, "Testing the Fruits: Aesthetics as Applied to Liturgical Media Art" (PhD diss., Union Theological Seminary, 2002), and James A. Fenimore, Jr., "High-Tech Worship: Digital Display Technologies and Protestant Liturgical Practice in the U.S." (PhD diss., Rensselaer Polytechnic Institute, 2009). Given the pace of technological advancements, such works quickly become dated as comprehensive guides.

13. Brian Blackmore, interview by Lester Ruth, September 9, 2016.

14. Michelle Makariak, e-mail to Lester Ruth, September 28, 2016.

into ten tracks: acoustics, audio, lighting, Internet, video, music, broadcasting, computers, drama, and general administration.[15]

Personnel changes began about the same time. By the late 1990s the list of who ought to be on such a staff, paid and unpaid, in a well-equipped church could be extensive: sound director, lighting director, floor director, overall coordination director, technical director, videographer, graphic artist, and engineers for audio, video, and computers.[16] The scope of technological consulting grew more complex in the 1990s, too. The A (audio) of consulting became AV (audio-visual) as churches grew interested not only in good sound but also in video, projection, and lighting. Eventually consultants have moved from that label to becoming integrators, considering the multiple dimensions involved in advanced worship technology.[17]

Since the late 1980s (with acceleration in the late 1990s), there has been increasing sophistication in worship technology. The acceleration has not slowed as ever-more sophisticated equipment becomes smaller, less expensive, and easier to use, bringing more equipment and possibilities into a wider range of churches. Let's consider the major developments over this time, beginning with sound.

Into the 1980s the sound systems used in congregations were often just speakers, a few microphones, and a small sound mixer in the pulpit. In the late 1980s and early 1990s, developing sound systems in movie theaters began to shape how sound could be done in worship spaces.[18] Moreover, in the1990s the increasing number of worship bands with their electronically amplified sound and multiple vocalists made necessary a more complex sound board (or mixing console). Consequently, by the late 1990s guides and conferences on implementing contemporary worship instructed churches about the logistics of equipment, placement, and use, as in a 1998 Vineyard Fellowship essay about "serving through sound."[19] Since then a good sound system has become foundational and the mixing console—now more likely to be digital and not analog—has become a spatial fixture across contemporary worship.

---

15. Robert Phillips, "Changes in Technology," *Southwestern Journal of Theology* 42, no. 3 (Summer 2000): 56.

16. Thomas E. Boomershine and Len Wilson, "The Work of Media Ministers" in *Worship Matters: A United Methodist Guide to Ways to Worship,* ed. E. Bryon Anderson (Nashville: Discipleship Resources, 1999), 2:71–73.

17. Chuck Walthall, interview by Lester Ruth, September 16, 2016.

18. Ibid.

19. Marianne Kleine, "Serving through Sound," in *All About Worship*, ed. Julie Bogart (Anaheim, CA: Vineyard Music Group, 1998).

Technology has impacted the complexity in making music, too. Chapter 2 has mentioned already the use of in-ear monitors by musicians. Technology has enriched the sound heard by the congregation. Multitracks allow sounds from instruments not actually played live in the service to be added to the music that the congregation hears. In addition, the use of Ableton Live software to facilitate the creation of music electronically has moved music-making in many congregations to a new technological sophistication. Consequently, laptops have become a critical part of the equipment in many worship bands as they lead worship.

Projection has also taken significant steps forward since the 1990s. Initially churches using projection used a portable overhead projector. Transparencies were laid on top and were switched out by hand. Other churches used slide projectors to show song lyrics and other media. While most systems were simple, some arrangements of slide projectors were complex. The system at Willow Creek Community Church probably pushed the boundary of what churches tried. Upgrading from its original two synchronized slide projectors, this church eventually had thirty projectors organized into groups of ten.[20] (It was 2001 before it made its media system fully digital.) While congregations could make their own transparencies and slides, various companies also sold these materials, advertising their products into the early 2000s.

While overhead and slide projectors lingered through the 1990s, books promoting contemporary worship continued to presume them well until the middle part of that decade. For example, Kathy and Tim Carson's 1997 book, *So You're Thinking about Contemporary Worship*, promoted the benefits of projecting lyrics using transparencies on an overhead projector. Not all agreed. The previous year Barry Liesch had advocated slide projectors rather than overheads because of their artistic possibilities.[21] Arguments for both of these older forms of projectors would soon be overwhelmed by LCD (liquid-crystal display) and DLP (digital light processing) projectors, both providing superior results to overheads or slides. Greater portability and decreasing costs made these new projectors feasible for many more congregations. Quickly they displaced overheads and slides as well as the CRT (cathode ray tube) projectors that a very few churches had installed in the 1980s, a shift that secular periodicals noticed by the early 2000s.[22] Sociologists of religion also noticed this

---

20. Crowley-Horak, "Testing the Fruits," 71.

21. Tim Carson and Kathy Carson, *So You're Thinking about Contemporary Worship* (St. Louis: Chalice Press, 1997), 73–74; Barry Liesch, *The New Worship: Straight Talk on Music and the Church* (Grand Rapids: Baker Books, 1996), 95.

22. Janné Fielding, "Display Technology for Churches," *Entertainment Design* (April 2001 Supplement): 9–11.

increase in liturgical projection as statistical surveys bore witness to its spread: 11.9 percent of American congregations used video projection equipment in 1998, 26.5 percent in 2006–2007, and 35.3 percent by 2012.[23]

Projection sophistication continues to increase for churches seeking cutting edge technology. Those wanting next generation technology can move to LCD or LED (light-emitting diode) displays. With the source of light and image in both cases coming from within the display, a mounted projector within the space is no longer necessary. Both can also produce greater brightness of display, meaning tight control of sunlight is less of a problem. Recently more congregations have enlarged the area upon which images and text are displayed. Since the early 2000s, for example, more congregations have been moving to a triple-wide screen/display arrangement: between the two screens on either side of the platform stage a larger third screen has been installed at the rear of the platform stage. A step beyond this configuration is the use of environmental projection in which the entire front of the worship space can become an area for display, enabling creative shifts in the tone and mood of the space.

A rapid development in worship-related computer graphics and projection software has accompanied the advancements in projection. Through the 1990s most churches relied upon PowerPoint software, which had been released in 1990 as part of Microsoft Office. Developed for other purposes, PowerPoint's limitations as liturgical software eventually showed, especially in its assumption that a series of slides will proceed in a predetermined linear sequence. When worship leaders wanted to follow an impulse to add in an unplanned song or spontaneously return to a song's chorus to sing again, PowerPoint's linear sequencing caused what so many of us have experienced: the computer graphics operator desperately trying to find what slide to project. Churches soon began desiring more capable software.

Answers emerged at the turn of the century. Development of projection software designed for contemporary worship often began with various conferences and rallies in the late 1990s or from churches with their own talented programmers. From Promise Keeper rallies, Fresh Air Media developed a program eventually marketed as SundayPlus.[24] Similarly, people associated with Josh McDowell's ministry tours created MediaShout and the staff associated with Passion conferences, ProPresenter. Churches could begin

23. The statistical information is from the Association of Religion Data Archives, accessed August 5, 2016, http://www.thearda.com/conQS/QS_254.asp.

24. James Fenimore, "Boys and Their Worship Toys: Christian Worship Technology and Gender Politics," *Journal of Religion, Media and Digital Culture* 1, no. 1 (January 2012): 11; accessed January 13, 2016, http://www.jrmdc.com.

purchasing these programs by the early 2000s along with other options like EasyWorship, SongShow Plus, and SongScreen Liquid, many deriving from programs developed for individual congregations. Market share among the major companies shifted in the mid-2000s as MediaShout distributed a PC version with bugs and delayed release of a Mac version. At the same time Pro-Presenter released a new version with a strikingly easy user interface. ProPresenter soon became the first choice for many congregations, especially after release of a Windows version in 2008–2009.[25]

These new presentation programs developed for worship allowed nonlinear sequencing of slides. In addition, as the programs grew more advanced, they allowed incorporation of a wide variety of media within the slides such as artistic backgrounds, motion backgrounds, and video. Not surprisingly companies selling worship-related computer graphics began in the early 2000s.

Projection involves magnifying light; it also involves controlling or suppressing other light to accentuate the magnification. Consequently, as projection became more standard and developed in the 1990s, so churches likewise grew more interested in complex lighting systems. The brightness limitations of early projectors increased the need for controlling light in the space, both natural and artificial. (Projectors emitting higher levels of brightness, measured in lumens, were more expensive.)

In addition, by the late 1990s, the growing influence of practices brought over from entertainment venues created desire to control light for artistic purposes. Even by 2000 a Baptist commentator on contemporary worship could note the growth of "professional lighting techniques with automated moving lights" as well as strobe lights, lasers, and fog machines (or hazers).[26] Soon considering lighting became a standard part of worship planning as some congregations planned in detail the order of worship with respect to lighting for mood and effect, often controlled through computers.

The cutting edge of lighting continues to develop both with respect to the lights themselves as well as projection and monitors. These advancements allow much greater use of natural light and glass in the overall architecture while preserving the brilliance of the image seen by the congregation. A 16 × 9 LED wall in one of the campuses of San Diego's Rock Church, for example,

---

25. Information on the development of projection software came from an interview by Lester Ruth with Stephen Proctor (October 18, 2013).

26. Phillips, "Changes in Technology," 57.

enabled this congregation to renovate a former car dealership with multistory glass walls on three sides into a usable contemporary worship space.[27]

Controlling lighting has become desirable not only to shape mood and facilitate projection but also because of the needs of cameras to capture the best video. Today in many churches cameras not only capture video for recording but for IMAG (image magnification) projection during the service, showing close-ups of musicians, worshippers, and the preacher on the screen, as well as for connection with remote campuses and viewers through web-based platforms. Of course, cameras in worship were not new to the late 1990s. Some churches have had TV ministries for decades and even small churches could record their services for distribution through free cable access channels. But since the latter half of the 1990s IMAG has become a more prevalent practice. A handy touchstone for this development is Church of the Resurrection's (a United Methodist megachurch in Kansas City) first acquisition of a camera in 1998.[28] Today it is common in technologically developed worship services to have multiple cameras used and coordinated by a director who decides which shot is projected to the screens.

Since the late 1990s technology in contemporary worship has exploded. In 2000, right at the first shocks of this explosion, one academic article made one of the tremendous understatements in the history of contemporary worship: "The ubiquitous overhead projector has found its way from the bowling alley to the classroom to the worship center."[29] It was not that the observation was wrong: overhead projectors had become widespread. It was that by 2000 liturgical technological advancements had already eclipsed the overhead and made it a dinosaur in a rapidly expanding world of worship technology. And what was true then has only become even more true.

CLASSIC LITURGICAL SPACES AND CENTERS WITHIN CONTEMPORARY WORSHIP

What have all these developments meant with respect to typical spaces for contemporary worship? How do contemporary worship spaces compare

27. Rachel Dawn Hayes, "Earthly Light," *Church Designer* (July–August 2016): 18–23.

28. Constance E. Stella, *Wiring Your Church for Worship* (Nashville: Abingdon Press, 2007), 65.

29. Phillips, "Changes in Technology," 58.

to historical forms of liturgical architecture? A schema developed by liturgical historian James White provides a useful grid for comparison.

According to White, most Christian worship has required six different liturgical spaces (i.e., meaning a distinct area within the building) and several related liturgical centers.[30] For White, the six liturgical spaces found in most historical forms of worship have been gathering, movement, congregational, choir, baptismal, and altar table. Gathering space was where a congregation assembled. Movement space was exactly that; think aisles in most cases. Congregational space was where rank-and-file worshippers sat and stood. Choir space was for musicians; the name chosen indicates White's presumption about who provided music. Baptismal and altar-table spaces were straightforward labels pointing to the areas in which baptism and the Lord's Supper were administered.

White's four liturgical centers pointed to specific furnishings: the baptismal font/pool, the altar table, the pulpit, and the presider's chair.[31] Like his labels for the different liturgical spaces, his names for these furnishings reflected common usage. Today only the presider's chair might raise questions. By this term White meant the special seat for the minister who preached and had the main responsibility for leading.

To fit a typical contemporary worship building, adaptations must be made to White's schema. Consider his six liturgical spaces. Of the six, only three are commonly found as standard in contemporary worship: gathering, movement, and congregational. But eliminating classic spaces is not the only story. The gathering space has become more important, for example, as congregations with contemporary worship have emphasized accessibility and hospitality. Thus many churches now contain attractive atriums outfitted with comfortable seating, information and welcome centers, bookstores, and coffee shops.

Of White's other historical spaces (choir, baptismal, and altar-table spaces), two need to be seen as only occasional (baptismal and altar table) in contemporary worship. Baptismal and altar-table spaces tend to be found only in churches that have placed their contemporary services in adapted sanctuaries or, if in newly constructed buildings, in congregations whose traditions place a high value on the Eucharist (e.g., Lutheran and Episcopalian) or baptism, especially by immersion (e.g., Baptist).

30. James F. White, *Introduction to Christian Worship*, 3rd ed. (Nashville: Abingdon Press, 2000), 86 87.

31. Ibid., 88–89.

The remaining space in White's historical schema, the choir space, must be reframed radically to fit contemporary worship. Although choirs are used in a few contemporary services, being contemporary in worship has meant revisiting the role and number of singers as well as the musical instruments played. Simply put, to consider the space for musicians is no longer a matter of determining where to place the choir, but involves front and center placement of the vocal ensemble surrounded by the ubiquitous band of guitars, keyboards, and drum kit. Therefore, it is no longer fitting to speak of a choir space in most cases of contemporary worship. The exceptions are those congregations that still incorporate a choir into their musical ensemble or those in which the contemporary service has been placed in an unadapted building. In the latter case, one often finds the choir space unused.

The better term to designate the musician-related space in contemporary worship is platform stage. Both labels (platform and stage) are used widely across contemporary worship. The platform stage is usually the most dominant architectural space at the front. Its centrality and height reinforces the significance of the musicians in the liturgical space and in the leadership of the service. We will use *platform stage* even when there is no elevation to the musician's space as sometimes happens in adapted spaces.

	STANDARD	OCCASIONAL
SPACES	gathering (G); movement (M) congregational (C); platform stage (PS)	baptismal (B) altar table (AT)
CENTERS	*PRESUMING INCREASING LEVELS OF TECHNOLOGY:* sound control (front of house booth) (sc) projection (screen/monitor (sm) and projector (pr) with computer graphics (cg) control) lighting control (lc) videography, including cameras (v) production room (pr)	baptismal font/pool (b) altar table (at) pulpit (p) presider's chair (pc)

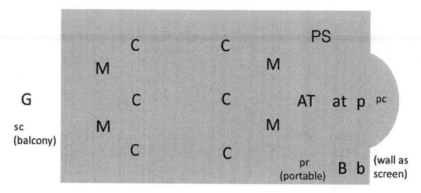

Contemporary worship inserted in a nineteenth-century sanctuary, Hillsborough United Methodist Church, Hillsborough, North Carolina

White's categories for liturgical centers also must be changed to fit contemporary worship. Furnishings for baptism and Communion are found only occasionally. That is true, too, for a pulpit as a liturgical center, especially for one that is fixed in place and substantial in size. Preachers tend to speak at congregational level or at the front of the platform stage, perhaps using stands or small tables moved on and off with ease for their notes and Bible. And in an overwhelming number of cases there is no special chair for the preacher (presider), who now sits with the congregation until time to speak.

Although all of White's original liturgical centers are marginal in contemporary worship, there are new, crucial liturgical centers. Not surprisingly, these liturgical centers of contemporary worship tend to be technological centers. The number of these technology-related centers depends on the level of technological advancement of a congregation. As technological sophistication increases, more liturgical centers are found.

The most basic and universal liturgical center is for sound control, most typically a sound mixing board (or console) located in a separated—yet open—area. (Sometimes this area is called the sound booth although it is not—and cannot be—totally enclosed.) In some churches this area might contain not only the controls for sound, but also other technological controls such as lighting. The area might be known as the front of house, a term drawn from spaces for performing arts to designate the portion of a venue that is open to the public. The operators in this center need to hear what the congregation experiences which is why sound (and lighting) control is placed here.

The next level of liturgical center in contemporary worship is projection. The screen (or monitor) is only one aspect to this liturgical center; the actual projector is another. And now, since digitalization of projection in the late 1990s, churches must consider where to place the computer graphics control. The actual location of the computer running graphics control can vary. Sometimes it is in the sound/front of house booth, sometimes in a side room near that booth, and sometimes in a separate production room.

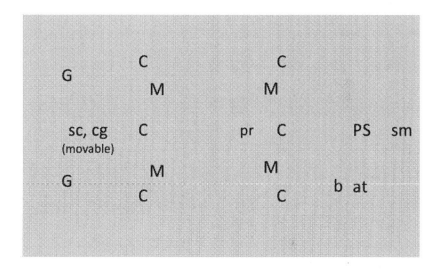

Contemporary worship in a multipurpose Christian Life Center, White Plains United Methodist Church, Cary, North Carolina

With increasing technological complexity some churches have a separate control for lighting, a third liturgical center. This control can be found in the front of house booth or in its own separate booth as long as the operator has visual access to the congregational space.

Videography is the next level of liturgical center. The central feature of this center is the camera. Placement can vary. Some are mounted on the building and remotely controlled. Others are fixed on stands and directly hand controlled; sometimes these cameras are on their own elevated platforms to give them line-of-sight over worshippers' heads. As congregations move up in technological sophistication, they utilize movable cameras either on remote controlled booms or handheld by roving operators.

Congregations using IMAG or streaming will need another liturgical center, the production room. The personnel and equipment in this room control and coordinate everything going to the screen, unless the computer graphics person is located in the front of house booth or elsewhere. A key piece of hardware in the production room will be the video switcher, used to select which camera shot will be fed to the projection system. The production room also controls remote streaming, unless a congregation separates the mixing for streaming to yet another room.

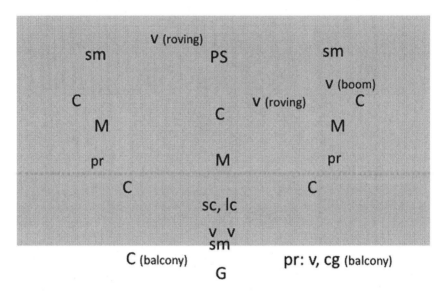

Arrangement of spaces and centers in a technologically advanced megachurch, New Hope Church, Durham, North Carolina

FLUIDITY OF SPACE IN CONTEMPORARY WORSHIP

Technological advancements in contemporary worship have introduced a fluidity in the notion of liturgical space itself, a relationship to space that is exceptional in the history of Christian worship.[32] One manifestation of this fluidity is the development of remote campuses linked to a central, main campus. Through the use of live or delayed streaming—or in

---

32. A rare historical example of supra-spatial fluidity is Bishop G. Bromley Oxnam simultaneously consecrating Communion by radio for 50,000 Methodists in 1,500 congregations on the 1938 bicentennial of John Wesley's "heartwarming" Aldersgate experience. See Robert Moats Miller, *Bishop G. Bromley Oxnam: Paladin of Liberal Protestantism* (Nashville: Abingdon Press, 1990), 193–94.

recordings—remote campuses can share worship with an originating campus, a practice advocated as early as 2003.[33] Commonly it is the sermon that is shared. A variation is the live streaming of a service into the gathering space or overflow room of a single campus. This technological linkage is a form of spatial connection.

The use of IMAG (image magnification) provides another aspect of fluidity: spatial collapse. Because the faces of musicians and preachers get magnified worshippers even at remote distances from the platform stage are able to see their facial expressions. The technology thus collapses the sense of distance between a worshipper and worship leader.

A third dimension of fluidity of space in contemporary worship deals with multiple liturgical spaces on a single campus in which there are simultaneous, independent services. Some churches divide worshippers by age with services geared for children to older teens. Other churches separate by language. Some do both, like Richmond Hill Christian Community Church in Toronto, with overlapping services for children, youth, Cantonese-speakers, Mandarin-speakers, and English-speakers.

Finally, technology can create fluidity within a single physical space and service. In congregations with fully developed technology, there are several sonic spaces occurring. The average worshipper hears from the main sound system. The musicians are privy to that sound, too, as well as anything else being fed into their in-ear monitors. And the multiple persons within the tech staff communicate with each other through their own headsets and microphones. What results is a triple-layered sonic space rare in earlier forms of Christian worship.

---

33. Bill Easum and Dave Travis, *Beyond the Box: Innovative Churches That Work* (Loveland, CO: Group, 2003), 85–103.

Chapter 4

THE MUSIC OF CONTEMPORARY WORSHIP: ORIGINS THROUGH THE 1980S

Without a doubt, music plays an important role in Christian worship throughout church history. But the perennial question has been this: exactly how important a role should it play? Since the establishment of the church in the early centuries, ecclesial leadership had sought to delineate the role and function of music in worship. As a result, music often was assigned a subservient role and its emotive character restrained. However, in contemporary worship there has been a shift. Music is in the driver seat in contemporary worship. Musicians hold a central spot not only in the physical space itself but also in the planning and leading of services. And, in addition, music's emotive character has been unleashed in contemporary worship.

But the history of music in contemporary worship is not only about a shift in the role and function of music in worship. It is also about the rise of new styles of worship music drawn from popular music. The mid-twentieth century was a time for important changes in forms of popular music. The 1960s, for instance, was the age of rock and roll, the Beatles (1960–1970), and Elvis Presley (1935–1977). It was a time when changes in the socio-cultural landscape were fueled and embodied by music making. In that era, music moved out of the concert hall to the dance hall and into homes via the airwaves of radio and television broadcasts. Advancement in technology ushered in electrical power to instruments and amplifiers. Principally, this led to the flourish of electric guitars, overdrive amplifiers, and electric Hammond organs vying to replace pipe organs, and the emerging of music recording studios that fueled music production. Equally significant in the 1960s was the development of rock band-based music dependent on electric guitar and drums. All these changes would have an impact on the music of contemporary worship.

At the same time there was a sense of despondency toward the status quo in society that gave rise to a countercultural ethos as seen in the various people movements such as the civil rights movement (1954–1968) and the hippie movement (mid-1960s). While some sought spiritual enlightenment in Eastern mysticism, others turned to the Jesus People movement in the late 1960s and early 1970s as a means of returning to "essential" Christianity without extraneous trappings. Early expressions of contemporary worship, as pointed out earlier in this book, sought to avoid the generic to-whom-it-may-concern approach but embraced the deep personal devotional and attachment to Jesus found in this movement. That approach played out in music, too. More often than not, it subtly invited listeners to come along on the authentic spiritual journey attested to by the singer. This quality, beyond the actual sound of the musical notes, was another way that early contemporary worship music drew upon popular music. Early contemporary worship songwriters followed the lead of secular parallels in the music of Pete Seeger ("Where Have All the Flowers Gone?"), Bob Dylan ("Blowin' in the Wind"), John Denver ("Take Me Home, Country Road"), and folk music groups like the Mamas and the Papas ("California Dreamin'") or Peter (Yarrow), Paul (Stookey), and Mary (Travers) ("Puff the Magic Dragon").

In this chapter, we will examine several key expressions of early contemporary worship music and their development from the mid-twentieth century through the 1980s. Our goal is not an exhaustive survey of contemporary worship music but a sampling of important milestones in its history to document the early changes in the role, function, and style of music in contemporary worship. A secondary goal is to give some hint of the breadth of this music, especially across racial lines.

THE MUSIC OF THE JESUS PEOPLE

A critical source for music in the early stages of contemporary worship was the new music written by the Jesus People movement. As in its cultural counterpart (the late 1960s hippie subculture), this movement created new worship that reflected the sound and spirit of pop music at that time. In terms of song lyrics, the Jesus People movement's spirituality was also largely dominated by the imminence of Christ's return as made popular by Hal Lindsey's *The Late Great Planet Earth*.[1] To that end, songs would often call

---

1. Hal Lindsey, *The Late Great Planet Earth* (Grand Rapids: Zondervan, 1970).

for prioritizing one's life to please God and to be prepared for the Second Coming of Jesus.

A good example was the popular song entitled "Seek Ye First," a song composed by Karen Lafferty. It—and the story of its composer—exemplified the ethos of the Jesus People that focused on faith and trust in God.[2] Although she had grown up in a Christian home and attended a Baptist church, a Christian friend helped Lafferty elevate her faith in 1970 when she began to "understand the glorious truth of walking daily with Jesus."[3] This happened even as she worked as a musician in a nightclub. As a result of her spiritual renewal, she began to witness to people in bars. (Jesus People were known for an ever pervasive public witness.) She also became more active in Calvary Chapel of Costa Mesa, California, a church growing quickly in its outreach to the hippie subculture of Southern California. There she began to sense a call to ministry, part of which was songwriting.

"Seek Ye First" reflects the musical template of early contemporary worship songs in their earliest phase. Broadly speaking, the music-making effort was generally folk-like in nature with minimal sophistication in instrumental or vocal amplification. Harmonic organization of songs was simple and typically stayed in primary chords of Tonic (I), Dominant (V), and Subdominant (IV). In nonmusician's terms, if the song key was in C major, as is the original key for the song, "Seek Ye First," chord (I) would be C-E-G, (V) G-B-D, and (IV) F-A-C. Occasionally, there would be the use of relative minor chords: A minor (VI, A-C-E, related to I), and E minor (III, E-G-B, related to V), which are found within the scale of C major.

In terms of lyrics, many early contemporary worship songs would be scripture verses set to music as with Lafferty's song. Matthew 6:33, "But seek ye first the kingdom of God, and his righteousness; and all these things shall be added unto you," (KJV) provided the core of this song's lyrics. There was minimal attempt to explicate the scriptures or furnish any introspective thoughts in this musical undertaking. These sorts of scriptural songs were simply select Bible verses set to music (hence it is fitting to refer to them as "scripture in song" or simply "scripture choruses") with simple accompaniment that typically features acoustic guitar, bass guitar, piano, and possibly simple drumming. Often times, accompaniment takes on a supporting role

---

2. For Lafferty's testimony about the creation and performance of the song: accessed August 16, 2016, https://youtu.be/7p9UN7DAmV4 and https://youtu.be/-8DADKDPQOo.

3. Karen Lafferty, "Biography," accessed August 16, 2016, http://www.musiciansformissions.com/KL/biography/. Other biographical information on Lafferty is drawn from this same site.

to the vocals. Typically, the song would first be sung either by a solo or in unison before variations were introduced. These can come in the form of part singing. In the 1974 "Seek Ye First" recording, only one verse and one chorus were recorded. Given the identical chords, both verse and chorus were then sung at the same time after the former was sung through by Karen Lafferty.

In terms of music structure, this verse-chorus approach was the primary form of contemporary worship song. In the next chapter, we will see that music devices such as prechorus, bridge, and segue were adopted to address the limitation of this verse-chorus structure.

Coincidentally, this back-to-the-scripture musical movement also occurred beyond the shores of North America. On the other side of the world, New Zealanders Dave and Dale Garrett also felt led by God to begin their music ministry in 1973 in setting scriptures to music through their recording label, Scripture in Song. Their work soon spread around the world, providing one of the first non-American musical sources for the early stages of contemporary worship in North America. The Garretts' goal was straightforward: just the writing and recording of scripture verses set to the contemporary music of the time, with a rhythm section (piano, guitar, and drums), all sounds that were unfamiliar to the church culture of the day but growing more familiar in popular culture.[4]

In the United States, the seedbed for this new soundscape was often found in the various Christian communes and independent churches in California. Principally important was the ministry of Pastor Chuck Smith at Karen Lafferty's church, Calvary Chapel in Costa Mesa. Although his ministry was instrumental in the birth of contemporary worship songs, there were three different musical expressions at Calvary Chapel where Smith ministered. Hymns were used on Sunday mornings, reflecting the congregation's previous practice as well as Smith's background as a Four Square Gospel pastor. Typically, there would be three hymns and they were accompanied by both organ and piano. For Sunday evening, the scripture song form in its folk music nuance was featured and sung unaccompanied. Smith thoughtfully sequenced these songs into a worship set as he himself led the congregation in singing. What resulted was a "seamless stream of song with his voice providing the strong melody for the congregation."[5] Lyrics were not provided, since

---

4. David and Dale Garrett, "The Garrett Family Story," accessed August 16, 2016, http://www.davidanddalegarratt.com/garrattfamilystory.html.

5. Charles E. Fromm, "Textual Communities and New Song in the Multimedia Age: The Routinization of Charisma in the Jesus Movement" (PhD diss., Fuller Theological Seminary, 2006), 186.

either the majority of the congregation would know the songs or they could be rapidly learned once introduced, due to their simple texts. Despite the simplicity of the songs, there was beauty, too, as the songs could be divided into parts for the congregation (often divided by male and female voices doing call and response) or sections of the auditorium participated in various refrains at different times to generate an antiphonal effect.

Despite its quick and growing emergence as a source for new songs, Calvary Chapel itself maintained an eclectic musical repertoire in worship. Cheryl Brodersen, Chuck Smith's daughter, who now leads the women's ministry of the church, describes the congregation's musical breadth:

> Sunday night worship was a mixture. Some of the songs could have been considered original. There were a lot of Scripture songs written by the hippies.... Those would have been mixed with choruses that were popular in the church like, "Everybody Ought to Know", "Oh, How I Love Jesus", "Amazing Grace"... and others. I know that Karen Lafferty, Debbie Kerner, and others wrote some of the Scripture songs we sang. I think dad (Chuck Smith) had a desire to really get the word into people, so the Scripture songs tended to be the most sung. We sang Galatians 2:20, Zephaniah 3:17, 1 Corinthians 13, Micah 6:8, Jeremiah 31:12, [which] are a few I remember vividly.... [Monday] was a time when those who received some type of song could just share it with the community of believers. Some of the songs became choruses we sang. Monday night was more like an open mic.... Usually, my dad had been approached by someone earlier in the week. They had played or sung for him and he invited them to share on Monday night. In those days the midweek study was not on Wednesday nights but Thursday evenings. My dad taught Sunday morning—sermons. Sunday night was a through-the-Bible study. Monday night was a more contemporary study and geared more toward the hippies and young people. It was very casual. It usually featured a band and the music was done with guitars. Sunday morning was hymns with piano and organ. Sunday evening was usually my dad singing acapella. [It was the] same with Thursday evenings.[6]

In this succinct snapshot of the worship services at Calvary Chapel, we see the development of two streams of music arising from the Jesus People movement: contemporary worship song, which was geared for congregational singing, and contemporary christian music (CCM), which steered toward concerts and albums and other forms of nonworship expression. At Calvary Chapel both coexisted with previous forms of evangelical worship that were hymn-based, especially in Sunday morning worship services.

---

6. Cheryl Brodersen, e-mail to Swee Hong Lim, January 15, 2016.

In addition to providing the liturgical home for Jesus People songwriters, Calvary Chapel was important in facilitating the recording of their new music. In 1971, Maranatha! Music was established out of this church and released its first album, *The Everlastin' Living Jesus Music Concert*. Smith established this nonprofit Christian recording label for the promotion of "Jesus music."

At Calvary Chapel one of the most prominent bands was Love Song. In describing its music, Chuck Girard (1943–), one of the band's founders, wrote that their music was "simple, direct, and anything but subtle in its message of the love of Jesus."[7] The band (minus one member who was in jail for marijuana possession) had shown up on a Monday and offered its services to Chuck Smith. Confessing that they had only been Christians for two weeks, Smith was cautious initially but he asked these hippies to play a bit for him. Hearing them play, Smith was overcome with a sense of God's Spirit and immediately asked them to play that night. The band agreed, noting their missing comrade would be released at 4 p.m. and therefore able to join them, too.[8]

From the beginning Love Song sought to write music that was fitting and authentic to themselves and to their fellow young Christians in the Jesus People movement. By design, music from this band was "contemporary in style," reflecting the popular music that they and their friends knew while also being "uncompromising in its content" according to the nature of their new evangelical faith.[9] Initially the sound was more acoustic, with the band members playing acoustic guitars, a violin, and bongos. Over time they moved toward electric instruments.

A technical analysis of their works quickly shows a musical sophistication beyond a basic harmonic progression of chords I, IV, V, and their relative tonalities. This sophistication contrasts with the simplicity of the contemporary worship songs written by other Jesus People for congregational singing. Overall Love Song's music featured the use of chord inversions, diminished chords, and secondary dominants.

Love Song's main emphasis was not on writing songs for congregational worship; nonetheless the group was influential in instilling a high-quality Christian musicianship that replicated the sounds of popular music. As Ralph

---

7. Chuck Girard, "Forward" for Dave Hollandsworth's website, One-Way.org (June 1997), accessed August 16, 2016, http://one-way.org/jesusmusic/.

8. Chuck Smith, "Calvary Chapel and the Music of the Jesus Movement 1969–1977," accessed August 16, 2016, https://youtu.be/oZZqtyYiVQQ.

9. Chuck Girard, "Love Song: The History," accessed August 16, 2016, http://one-way .org/lovesong/history6.htm.

Carmichael (himself a noted musician of Christian rock) put it, Love Song's music "had a purity and authenticity that captured the attention of an entire generation." Likewise Carmichael notes the group's wider impact: "I feel certain they laid the groundwork for the whole worship and praise phenomenon that has permeated the church music scene today!"[10]

The commercial viability of this Contemporary Christian Music was not lost on the secular music recording industry or entrepreneurial Christians willing to create their own labels. One of the earliest was Maranatha! Music, a company originating in Chuck Smith's Calvary Chapel. Through the 1970s, Maranatha! released albums featuring worship-related songs as well as other albums featuring popular contemporary Christian artists. To Maranatha!'s leadership it seemed as if the resources needed to promote the individual artists kept increasing with diminishing results while their projects focusing on simple songs of worship flourished. By 1980 that leadership had made a decision, releasing the nonworship artists from contractual obligations and focusing instead on efforts to equip young musicians for leading worship in local congregations.[11]

That decision has proved to be an important one in the history of contemporary worship. This refocusing effort by Maranatha! led to the strengthening of an emerging genre of contemporary worship songs intended for congregational use. In that vein the label produced a series of albums starting in 1974 entitled Maranatha! *Praise*.[12] The first track of its first *Praise* album featured the song, "Praise the Lord."[13]

This album was produced by Tommy Coomes, a member of Love Song. Vocalists like Chuck Girard and others from the same band were featured in a few tracks. They were listed as the Maranatha! Praise Band in the recording. In examining the album, one can discern the early schema of contemporary worship song. The texts typically expressed personal devotion to Jesus or God while the music was not overly sophisticated in arrangement. For the opening number, "Praise the Lord," the song began with simple guitar plucking of chords I and V that ushered in the vocalists accompanied by simple drumming of a "straight" rock beat pattern. This approach enabled

---

10. Ralph Carmichael, "Excerpts from Carmichael's Exposition on Jesus Music," in Fromm, "Textual Communities and New Song in the Multimedia Age," 369.

11. Charles E. Fromm, "New Song to Contemporary Christian Music Entertainment" (master's thesis, Fuller Theological Seminary, 1996), 73–74.

12. *The Praise Album*, Maranatha! Music, 1974, 33 1/3 rpm.

13. Words and music by Chuck Girard, Fred Field, Herb Brendlin, Jay Truax, and Tommy Coomes. An audio sample of this song is available at https://youtu.be/svaTu857YqU.

the drumming to serve as the "track" tempo pulse. For the chorus, the entry of a piano obbligato line of step-wise half note pulse offered the next level of melodic enhancement. The bass combined with an intricately played piano in arpeggio style tracks with other instruments ushered in the second verse that adds rhythmical complexity to the song. The third verse used nonlexical syllables of "la la la" and "ah" thereafter returning to the singing of the chorus. The song ended with a gradual fade out through eight repetitions of the first stanza with the instruments improvising. Sonically speaking, the instrumentation did not overpower the vocal lines and there was understanding of sonic layering where instruments were strategically added in the accompaniment of the song in order to heighten the emotive property of the song. The abandonment of the lyrics and the use of nonlexical syllables as the third stanza was the high point of the song.

This instinct of creating a high point structure within the song was unique and unlike older hymns, which was a way in which the music of contemporary worship replicated the style of popular forms of music. For hymns, the high point is constructed within the strophic melody and is experienced in the repeated singing of the melody. The high point is usually short-lived and over in a measure or two. It is not tenable to musically stretch the climactic moment once it has come to pass. This stretching was quite different for contemporary worship songs since a high point could be readily extended with minimal disruption to lyrical consideration. To that end, there was no discernible attempt to create a high point in the melody for the song "Praise the Lord." Rather, the high point was crafted through the variation of instrumentation and vocal color to fulfill that emotive objective. Thus rather than a specific musical spot, a specific musical phrase when repeated several times served as the means of sustaining the high point. This particular undertaking was unique to the new genre of contemporary worship song.

The second song of the 1974 *Praise* album, "Father, I Adore You,"[14] took a different road although it had a similar schema of a simple start and ending simple with a complex middle section. It begins with a piano introduction using the chords of the song, G – Am7 – D – G – Em7 – C – D – G, with the voices singing in unison throughout the song. Through repetitions, it used two-part, then three-part singing. The song culminated with three parts canonic singing repeating all the verses before the last vocal part quietly ended the song accompanied by the piano.

---

14. Words and Music by Terrye Coelho. Audio sample of this song available at https://youtu.be/WYFtAfyF75k.

Without a doubt, simple devotional or scriptural song would be an apt description for this genre in its early stage of development. The vocal lines were consistently in the foreground and the recordings were relatively "clean" and acoustically driven without discernible electronic enhancement or manipulation.

AFRICAN AMERICAN DEVELOPMENTS IN THE 1960s AND 1970s

Within the African American congregational song world, there was also a corresponding development in the 1960s. Within the civil rights movement came protest songs that had roots in the black music of jazz, folk, rhythm and blues as well as gospel. Such genres readily migrated between worship and civil rights movement rallies. Examples of these songs include "We Shall Not Be Moved," "Go, Tell It on the Mountain," "Lift Every Voice and Sing," and "We Shall Overcome." The ability for genres of black music (and musicians) to migrate between different spheres of life started early. For instance, Thomas A. Dorsey, considered the father of gospel music, was able to cross from blues to gospel early in the twentieth century. At mid-twentieth century, Andraé Crouch did likewise and crossed between both sacred-secular genres of music making and also between the genres of gospel and songs for contemporary worship. One instance came in his first album with The Disciples released in 1970, a song entitled "The Blood Will Never Lose Its Power."[15] This was the first song he wrote, when he was fourteen years old.[16]

Again, the vocal lines were prominently showcased with accompaniment in the background. Bass guitar and drums provided rhythm and low register support. The use of vibraphone and Hammond Electric Organ as well as the call and response vocal line demonstrated the continuing influence of black gospel music culture in this emerging African American contemporary worship song genre. Textually, despite its confessional stance, its focus was overtly devotional and individualistic. Harmonically speaking, this song was sophisticated and used relative tonalities, chord inversions, and dominant 7ths with ease as it drew on its gospel music heritage. Consistent with that style, the vocal and bass lines upheld their improvisatory character. In terms of achieving

---

15. Words and music by Andraé Crouch. Audio sample available at https://youtu.be /eaASM4KZVzU.

16. Boyd Matson, video interview with Andraé Crouch (April 2011), accessed August 16, 2016, https://youtu.be/65x-skfsD0w.

a high point, this song used choral part singing to denote this element. Again unlike traditional hymns, the high point was not identifiable by a specific melodic spot but the manner in which the song was performed at a given point in the musical structure. A quick perusal of the song clearly indicated that the phrase "the blood that gives me strength from day to day, it will never lose its power," found in both the verses and the chorus, was important even though its melodic and harmonic organization remained unchanged regardless of where it occurs in the song. But by its performance practice, one can readily identify that the high point structure occurred in the chorus with dramatic changes to the vocal and instrumental arrangements. This was—and remains—the distinctive character of contemporary worship song: the performance practice of the song is critically determinative in creating the high point structure. This particular understanding also had an impact on understanding flow in worship and the arrangement of songs into sets for worship settings.

DEVELOPING WORSHIP SONG SETS IN THE 1980S

As noted in chapters 2 and 8, a variety of factors combined in the late 1970s and throughout the 1980s to create a sense of an extended time of congregational singing, that is, a worship set, as a standard feature of contemporary worship. Not surprisingly, recordings of contemporary worship songs from the 1980s began to reflect this development. Maranatha! Music's earlier *Praise* albums, for example, had one worship song recorded after another without a specific worship context. In contrast, the first album of Hosanna! Music (a recording label of Integrity Music Group) entitled *Behold His Majesty* (Hosanna! Music, 1983) was recorded at Grace World Outreach in St. Louis. Its producers elected to use the concept of a live worship event as a platform for their rendition. The result was an album consisting of twenty-five songs with a total duration of 61'05".[17]

In the playlist, we observe that the songs were integrated as a worship set with brief moments of encouraging exhortation, scripture acclamations, moments of prayer by the worship leader-musician, and occasional ecstatic responses of the congregation heard in the background. Secondary individual soloists were also called upon to complement the primary worship

---

17. Audio sample accessed August 16, 2016, https://youtu.be/cl6ArZuOKKI. Through the 1980s and 1990s Hosanna! cassette tapes were a major source of contemporary worship music to American churches, especially through Integrity's direct-to-consumer music club.

leader-musician in the recording. The first group of songs had a thematic focus of celebratory praise typified by a collective fast tempo in a common key of D major ending with a modulation to F major before the set ends. Having common tempo and tonality afforded flexibility and ease of song transition in a medley setting. To that end, the constituting songs of the set were not permanent fixtures and could be relocated within the set depending on the thematic focus of the grouping. After all, the worship climax was not dependent on the musical character of an individual song but on the structure of the set and its performance practice. It was equally astute for the producers to begin the album with the song "Majesty." Just as a plane requires a runway to attain its flight speed, the opening song had a similar musical function of raising the tempo while using the song to gather the congregation as a worshipping assembly.

For the duration of songs 7–14, there was a change of tempo. This could well be a set that focused on devotional worship, based on the keys of E major, D major, and C major. The relatively slower tempo made for easy key changes and intimate engagement of songs for an evocative worship experience. Another set grouping would be songs 15–16 with the reprise of the former in a quicker tempo. This set offered a different worship character that conveyed a sense of affirmation that could easily replace a sung doxology. Songs 17–20, given their minor tonality, formed the next song medley. Song 21 stood alone given its extended length of play. The album then closed with a grouping of four songs that began in D♭ major and modulated to E♭ major before ending. Here it is important to keep in mind that even though the song "Joy to the Lord" had a beats per minute (bpm) of 118, its pulse or *tactus* remained aligned to the other three songs that had a lower bpm of 83.[18] This set of songs drew on the verses of a familiar carol to declare the reign of God. Its declarative stance concluded with the last song entitled "Praise the Name of Jesus." This song recapitulated the overall theme of the album that Jesus was the focal point of this worship event. Like so much of contemporary worship, the liturgical focus sought to love on Jesus.

The songs on this album drove the worship set through the tempos, keys, and song lyrics. As described in chapter 2 a worship set with good flow often requires minimal spoken narrative by the worship leader to engage participants. Using familiar and singable songs, as in this case, increased the level of congregational participation. Indeed, this approach explicitly and sonically situated the worshipper into a vibrant sonic worship-experience setting that

---

18.   For a brief explanation of *tactus* in music, read John Jahr, "Tactus and Tempo," http://preludemusicplanner.org/2012/07/tactus-and-tempo/.

is fluid and emotive rather than being a passive listener of a series of songs without context. This album's strategy reflected an opportunity of active participation of singing in a thematically focused worship accompanied by rich orchestral music. Even though purchasers of the album might not have the same level of music making in their congregations, recorded and studio-produced albums have allowed listeners a type of virtual, aural-based worship experience regardless of where the listeners are situated.[19]

Hosanna! Music's initial album was not the only one showing what 1980s-era worship sets could be. In 1989, the West Angeles Church of God in Christ recorded the first volume of a series of CDs entitled *Saints in Praise*.[20] Scholars have noted this undertaking as an influential marker for the development of contemporary worship sets within African American churches.[21] Kenneth Ulmer, for example, describes how *Saints in Praise* not only reflected the emerging contemporary practice of this church, it provided an influential template that shaped the practice of other black congregations. He observed that the music-making effort at West Angeles Church of God in Christ promoted the "praise and worship" genre as de facto musical structure in African American Christian worship with the praise team overshadowing the choir as the driving force. He noted,

> Worship was now significantly reordered. Instead of the block upon disconnected block style of the tradition, there was now a "flow." In this reordering, worship is intended to be a continuum—rather than climbing higher and higher from one segment to the next—with worship flowing as seamlessly as possible from glory to glory.[22]

---

19.   For a discussion on the process of music making in forming virtual community, read Swee Hong Lim, "Methodologies of Musicking in Practical Theology: Portal into the World of Contemporary Worship Song," *International Journal of Practical Theology*, 18, no. 2 (2014): 305–16, especially 314–15.

20.   West Angeles Church of God in Christ Mass Choir and Congregation, *Saints in Praise*, vol. 1, directed by Patrick Henderson, recorded March 23, 1989 (The Sparrow Corporation, 1989), compact disc.

21.   Deborah Smith Pollard, *When the Church Becomes Your Party: Contemporary Gospel Music* (Detroit: Wayne State University Press, 2008), 26; Birgitta J. Johnson, "'This Is Not the Warm-Up Act!' How Praise and Worship Reflects Expanding Musical Traditions and Theology in a Bapticostal Charismatic African American Megachurch" in *The Spirit of Praise: Music and Worship in Global Pentecostal-Charismatic Christianity*, ed. Monique M. Ingalls and Amos Young (University Park: Pennsylvania State University Press, 2015), 121.

22.   Kenneth C. Ulmer, "Transformational Worship in the Life of a Church" in *Worship That Changes Lives: Multidisciplinary and Congregational Perspectives on Spiritual Transformation*, ed. Alexis D. Abernethy (Grand Rapids: Baker Academic, 2008), 184–85.

In other words, *Saints in Praise* reflected a developing sense of flow in and purpose of worship sets that was emerging in white Pentecostal churches at the same time.

In this album, the songs were formed into a playlist set organized by the three medleys of celebration, praise, and worship. Different tempos (as reflected in their bpm—beats per minute) were clearly sung in the different medleys. The celebration portion was faster compared to either the praise or worship segments. In musical terminology, the celebration portion was *allegro* (lively and fast), the praise medley being *andante* (a moderate pace), and the worship segment gauged as *adagio* (slow). As noted earlier, having a uniform *tactus* within the set facilitates the transition of songs in the set. Thus a worship leader could have shuffled the individual songs within the set and not lost integrity of the set so long as the tempo and key was maintained. The placement of the songs was thus a means to parlay the thematic focus. Therefore the choice to end with "In the Name of Jesus," culminating in a dramatic slowing down of the song on the last phrase, "Oh, tell me who can stand before us when we call on that great name! / Jesus, Jesus, precious Jesus, we have the victory," and emphatically singing the phrase "we have the victory," sought to confidently lay claim to life's success made possible through the power of Jesus.[23] Even though the basic dynamics of the set on this album reflected those more broadly in contemporary worship at that time, this congregation's music nonetheless expressed the rich and complex harmonic character that typifies the African American music tradition drawn from its Gospel roots.

In this chapter, we have situated the contemporary worship song genre in the context of the 1960s and looked at its development from its beginning in scripture-based songs to its effort of showcasing live worship—and actual worship sets—through recorded albums. These 1980s-era albums demonstrate the dynamics and flow of extended times of congregational singing. In addition, by production and promotion these albums enabled worshippers not part of these specific congregations to have access to the effervescent expressions of contemporary worship of churches with a well-endowed music ministry. All that was needed was access to Christian bookstores or a subscription to a direct mailing Christian music club. The stage was set for a massive expansion of contemporary worship in the next decade, including an explosion of its musical dimension.

---

23. West Angeles Church of God in Christ Mass Choir and Congregation, "Celebration Medley," in *Saints in Praise*, audio sample at 6'05"–6'30," accessed August 16, 2016, https://youtu.be/-F54OylH_dQ.

THE MUSIC OF CONTEMPORARY WORSHIP: 1990S TO THE PRESENT

Aside from the influence of a few British bands like the Beatles and the Rolling Stones, American popular music had dominantly influenced the rest of the world prior to the 1990s. The same can be said for contemporary worship: Maranatha! Music and Hosanna! Music left the most dominant imprints on the soundscape of contemporary worship's music. However, as happened in the world of popular music, this dominance changed in the 1990s when a distinct shift occurred in the character of songs and music making in contemporary worship. Since the mid-1990s large changes in the nature of contemporary worship's songs and in the sound of its music have continued. Many of these changes can be attributed to two foreign sources: England and Australia.

In this chapter we will describe the changing nature of contemporary worship music since the 1990s, drawing attention to the non-American influences as well as our own internal developments. While we will be examining the macro view of music making in the contemporary worship world in this chapter by highlighting key markers, we need to underscore that some of these practices would not have been found in all local congregations given the richer range of resources used in the recordings we reviewed for this chapter. In particular, the highly skilled worship team (musicians, vocalists, technical crew, sophisticated audio equipment, etc.) needed to reproduce what was being promoted by the Christian music industry and trendy worship conferences. Inevitably, the dawn of the twenty-first century witnessed the disconnect in contemporary worship: recordings of contemporary worship songs, which had served as a pedagogical and inspirational tool in promoting contemporary worship songs in the early years, eventually became much more of a showcase of talent. Whether the products were studio crafted or live worship event recordings, they reveal that the disconnect between congregations and the recorded artifacts deepened. Nonetheless these recordings provide useful ways to see larger trends in the songs and music of contemporary worship even as we remain aware of what they cannot tell us about music making at the grass roots level.

THE BRITISH INVASION

Appropriating a term used to describe an earlier infusion of United Kingdom-based music into the American pop scene, ethnomusicologist Monique Ingalls has labelled a similar spread of worship music from across the Atlantic as contemporary worship's own form of British Invasion. According to Ingalls, the contemporary worship world in America was ripe for invasion by the late 1990s. The growing popularity of contemporary worship in that decade had nonetheless created much conflict in the so-called worship wars. With music as a standard frontline in the battles, the songs and sound of contemporary worship in America had become deeply associated with internal strife. Toward the end of the decade Nashville based contemporary worship music producers encountered the music of British contemporary worship. To them the British songs not only represented a new sound but music executives "saw British worship music as a product of an embattled community in a secular community whose trials have unified them across lines of theological persuasion and stylistic preferences."[1] Put simply, the songs offered a vision of a renewed, fresh form of Christianity.

Once the British songs began to appear in America, their popularity grew quickly. In 1995, for example, British songwriter Graham Kendrick's song, "Shine, Jesus, Shine"[2] was ranked twenty-third by the US-based Christian Copyright Licensing International (CCLI) in its October report. This was the first time that a British song made it into the top twenty-five CCLI chart. Within five years, the song rose to become number 7. By 2003, there were five British songs in the top twenty-five: "Come, Now Is the Time to Worship" (Brian Doerksen), "I Could Sing of Your Love Forever," (Martin Smith), "The Heart of Worship" (Matt Redman), "Shine, Jesus, Shine" (Graham Kendrick), and "Better Is One Day" (Matt Redman). In 2008, the num-

---

1. Monique M. Ingalls, "A New Day of Worship: Transnational Connections, Musical Meaning, and the 1990s 'British Invasion' of North American Evangelical Worship Music," in *The Oxford Handbook of Music and World Christianities*, eds. Suzel Reily and Jonathan Dueck (Oxford: Oxford University Press, 2016), 433.

2. Words and music by Graham Kendrick. A video sample available at https://youtu.be /QGmT4Gsh8CU.

ber of British songs increased to eight. This number included two songs that ranked number 2 and 3 in the top twenty-five list reporting period. They were "Here I Am to Worship" (Tim Hughes) and "Blessed Be Your Name" (Matt Redman) respectively.[3] Since the Invasion of the late 1990s, a growing presence of British-crafted music in American contemporary worship has been unquestionable. Even as we have written this book, Redman's song "10,000 Reasons" has dominated the top of the most current lists.

The songs from across the pond were different from American songs. Like many of Kendrick's songs, the lyrics of "Shine, Jesus, Shine" were theologically articulate; it clearly delineated the various roles of Jesus rather than being self-absorbed. Some musicologists have noticed parallels between this song and sentiments in Charles Wesley's eighteenth-century hymn, "Love Divine, All Loves Excelling."[4]

Musically speaking, Kendrick's harmonic organization of "Shine, Jesus, Shine" was straightforward. He used chords I (G major), IV (C major), V (D major), and their relative minor tonalities: VI (E minor), II (A minor), III (B minor) as had early contemporary worship music songs described in chapter 4. However, the use of a chromatic mediant (F major) (flat VII) chord as substitution for A minor (relative minor of IV) on the last line of the stanza is rather striking.

Graham Kendrick was the vanguard of a generation of British songwriters whose works greatly impacted American contemporary worship.[5] Quickly rising to importance after the start of the Invasion in the 1990s was the work of British songwriter Matt Redman, particularly his 1998 song, "The Heart of Worship."[6]

Redman composed that song as a personal response to his youth pastor's challenge for the group to refocus on worshipping in a way that was not prop (i.e., music) dependent. This song was then sung at the then-Anglican Church plant, Soul Survivor Watford, crystallizing the call for the congregation to prioritize "unadorned" worship that demonstrated their devotion to

---

3. Ingalls, "A New Day of Worship," 426.

4. C. Michael Hawn, *History of Hymns: "Shine, Jesus, Shine"* (Nashville, TN: Discipleship Ministries), accessed August 15, 2016, http://www.umcdiscipleship.org/resources/history-of-hymns-shine-jesus-shine.

5. Further reading on Graham Kendrick's contribution to congregational song, see Bert Polman, "Songs for the Season: Introducing Graham Kendrick," in *Reformed Worship* (March 1996), http://www.reformedworship.org/article/march-1996/introducing-graham-kendrick.

6. An audio sample of the song was accessed August 15, 2016, https://youtu.be/P-Zp586pvZg.

God.[7] Redman did not expect this song to resonate with people beyond his local church context but it did.

THE AUSTRALIAN INVASION

The second source that shaped American contemporary worship song since the 1990s has been the music from Hillsong Church in Australia.[8] Established in 1983, this Pentecostal church came to the world's limelight through its music recording efforts in the 1990s. By the early 2000s, it dominated the contemporary worship soundscape not only in Australia and America but also around the world. That emergence as a global name brand of contemporary worship music occurred during the tenures of Geoff Bullock (1985–1995) and then Darlene Zschech (1995–2007) as Hillsong's music directors. Under Bullock, for example, a total of six albums were produced. Particularly well known was the song, "The Power of Your Love" (1992).[9]

This song became the title track for an album released in 1992, the first of many live worship recordings that Hillsong Church has released over the years. However, it was not the first recording effort of the church; that honor belonged to two studio albums: *Spirit and Truth* (1988) and *Show Your Glory* (1990).[10] *The Power of Your Love* album consisted of sixteen songs composed primarily by Bullock and rendered by the music team at Hillsong.

What was immediately striking in this album was the centrality of the full fervor rock-music character in their fast-paced music set. Hard-drumming and distorted-sounding electric guitars had prominent roles

7. The background of the song's creation as described by Matt Redman can be found in an interview with the British Broadcasting Corporation, https://www.youtube.com/watch?v=m83TSHhg-jU, and also in his interview with Canon J. John, https://www.youtube.com/watch?v=sh7ge--1Sws (24'00"- 26'25"). Both sites were accessed August 15, 2016.

8. For a brief historical account of Hillsong Church and its music-making experience, read Tanya Riches and Tom Wagner, "The Evolution of Hillsong Music: From Australian Pentecostal Congregation into Global Brand," *Australian Journal of Communication*, 39, no. 1 (June 2012): 17–36, and Tanya Riches, "The Evolving Theological Emphasis of Hillsong Worship (1996–2007)," *Australasian Pentecostal Studies* 13 (2010): 87–133.

9. Words and music by Geoff Bullock. An audio sample of the song in its original recorded key of Bb major, accessed August 15, 2016, https://www.youtube.com/watch?v=4EGxEG7LYZs.

10. Hillsong Music, *Who Is Hillsong Music Australia?*, accessed August 15, 2016, https://distribution.hillsong.com/help/about.

in driving the Hillsong worship experience. This musical quality stood in dramatic contrast from the production efforts of Maranatha! Music that shaped their projects toward a mild rock groove or the rich sonorous orchestral texture in Hosanna! Music (see chapter 4). So it is not surprising then that with Hillsong's focus of ministering to youths and young adults, its robust rock-music style became its signature. This was further accentuated in and through the Hillsong United (youth-focused) album series when it was launched in 1998.

In examining the live worship Hillsong album, *The Power of Your Love*, for its tempo map, it is possible to identify musical sets by relating the various sections to the tempo of the songs. Jubilant praise corresponds with quick tempo of bpm 170 and above. Indeed, the first six songs of the album *The Power of Your Love* appear to follow this guideline. Its fast pace and pulsating rhythm hold this section together. Introspective worship would bear a moderate tempo of bpm 100 or lower. Not surprising, we also find a group of songs having this characteristics present in the album.

Clearly, the tempo of the recorded live congregational performance of these songs was a key element in demarcating musical sets for the album. As such, the live album was not merely a collection of individual songs but a model demonstrating how the select songs could be sequenced for worship.

Commenting on the tempo range of the music created between 1996 and 2007 under Darlene Zschech's tenure, Tanya Riches, a songwriter and worship leader associated with Hillsong, provides helpful background information on Hillsong's early performance practices. In her research, she noted that there are four tempo sets that are aligned to their worship pattern between 1996 to 2010:[11]

200 .... 130 .... 99........................... 80.......... 55
| Up-Tempo Praise | Mid-Tempo Praise | Anthemic Worship | Slow Worship |

Hillsong's practice reinforces the emphasis as described in chapter 2 on tempo as a key element in creating a sense of flow in a worship set. According to Riches, "[Hillsong's] 'praise and worship' usually consisted of two faster and two slower songs and almost always lasts for twenty minutes."[12] The spectrum from "up-tempo" to "mid-tempo" to "anthemic" to "slow" as

---

11. Riches, "The Evolving Theological Emphasis of Hillsong Worship," 92.

12. Ibid., 92.

seen in Riches's graph above reflected the typical progress through tempos in a Hillsong worship set. And, as described in chapter 2, tempo was not the only consideration as Hillsong worshipped in congregational song. Riches describes other common practices:

> Songs flow between key (tonality) changes, causing minimal distraction to the congregation, as the band moves seamlessly through musical interludes and the congregation vocalizes their own prayers and praises to God, singing or speaking quietly in tongues (glossolalia).[13]

Hillsong's invasion of the global contemporary worship world began especially after Darlene Zschech became the church's music director in 1995. The church's guitar-driven, full-rock music-making style made an impact on American contemporary worship both in terms of songwriting and in terms of the leading of services. Similar impulses from the British Invasion reinforced this turn toward full rock in much of American contemporary worship. This new sound of contemporary worship music reverberated across both the Pacific and the Atlantic to reach American congregations. A major step forward occurred when Integrity Publishing began distributing Hillsong productions globally. That distribution began with Hillsong's album *Shout to the Lord* in 1996. It contained twelve songs featuring notable Hillsong music leaders such as Darlene Zschech, Geoff Bullock, and others.[14]

Subsequently, Integrity's marketing strategy positioned Zschech as the first female worship leader. Without a doubt, the riffing vocal style of Zschech—similar to that of a gospel singer—in her song, "Shout to the Lord" (1993)[15] became an emblem of Hillsong Church for its wider global constituency in the 1990s. By Hillsong's pastor's own estimate, thirty-five million Christians every week were singing that song in 2005.[16]

---

13. Ibid., 92–93.

14. Audio playlist accessed August 15, 2016, https://www.youtube.com/playlist?list=PL _3AnvpC0qofzZIojj7Cae9E4AF1u6SdM.

15. Words and music by Darlene Zschech. A video is available at https://www.youtube .com/watch?v=-qkNthzidLE.

16. C. Jones, *Australian Story—The Life of Brian (Brian Houston)*, (Australian Broadcasting Company, 2005), listed at https://www.abccommercial.com/librarysales/program/austra lian-story-life-brian-brian-houston; see also Riches and Wagner, "The Evolution of Hillsong Music," 23.

ENGLISH-SPEAKING AMERICAN DEVELOPMENTS

Even as these two musical invasions flowed into the United States, American congregations in the 1990s were enthralled with a song, "Lord, I Lift Your Name on High," written in 1989 by American songwriter Rick Founds.[17] In the annals of CCLI, this song bears the distinction of being the most popular song within the American contemporary worship song corpus. It was the number one song in CCLI's (US) database from April 1995 through April 2002 and was covered by many groups in diverse musical styles. In CCLI's twice-a-year top twenty-five song lists, first compiled in 1989, no song has appeared more often than this song. It appeared on thirty-seven consecutive lists over eighteen and one-half years. In addition, no other song can rival its run as the number one song: fifteen consecutive six-month periods. Not surprising, "Lord, I Lift Your Name on High" was equally popular overseas, a fact seen in the CCLI reports from the United Kingdom and Australia. In America, much of its initial popularity came from its use in the Promise Keepers rallies of the late 1990s. The men who sang it there carried it back to their home churches.

Founds's song was an example of a common source for the writing of contemporary worship songs, namely the personal devotional and prayer life of the songwriter. In this song's case, the fusion of his reflection on the life and work of Christ merged with what he was thinking when reading about hydraulics and the different states of water. The scientific explanation of water's movement (a cycle from condensation to precipitation to absorption by the earth to nourish plants, which release it back to the air) provided a way of contemplating the gracious movements of Christ in his work of salvation. The fusion of scientific and devotional reflection led to the soon-familiar lyrics of the song.[18]

Stylistically speaking in its original recording, Founds's musical approach maintained the Maranatha! Music normative signature of a singable melody girded by foundational harmonic writing and mild rock groove within the long standing verse–chorus song form of contemporary worship song that had been standard up to this point. Its distinctive character laid in the lyrical

---

17. Words and music by Rick Founds. An audio sample available at https://youtu.be/jFoMK49H0Oc.

18. Rick Founds, "The Story Behind: Lord I Lift Your Name on High" in *Rick Founds Music*, accessed August 15, 2016, http://rickfounds.com/images/Lord_I_Lift_Your_Name_On_High-Song_Story.pdf.

content that credibly articulated the personhood and salvific work of Christ. This theological remembrance of Christ's work coupled with a multitude of covers by various artists generated and sustained its popularity across several years.

Notwithstanding the popularity of this individual song, the late 1990s would see the emergence of a generation of young American songwriters who would soon become household names in the world of contemporary worship songs. Chris Tomlin has been foremost among the new American writers and performers with songs such as "How Great Is Our God" (2004) and "Amazing Grace (My Chains Are Gone)" (2008), which have earned him numerous awards. "How Great Is Our God,"[19] cowritten by Ed Cash and Jesse Reeves, was one of Tomlin's breakthrough hits.

Distinctively speaking, "How Great Is Our God" exemplified a development in the contemporary worship song musical form. It transitioned away from the earlier verse-chorus of the 1980s, taking on a more complex structure that includes the use of a bridge. This 2004 song was an example of a wider phenomenon occurring more frequently in the contemporary worship songs since the 1990s. Beginning with the song "I Could Sing of Your Love Forever" (1994), which was one of the earliest contributions of the British Invasion, contemporary worship songs in the 1990s have incorporated structures that involved more than verses and choruses. (Note that many of the earliest songs in this genre were chorus only.) Tomlin's song incorporated a bridge. Subsequent songs might include prechoruses, special endings, and interludes.[20]

In the field of music theory, there are specific functions associated with musical structures.[21] In essence, the introduction of these new forms sought to address the compositional problem of ebb and flow in musical energy as well as familiarity and contrast in musical perception. Musicologist Mine Dogantan-Dack observes,

19. Words and music by Chris Tomlin, Ed Cash, and Jesses Reeves.

20. For more detailed information on the rise of more complex musical structures in contemporary worship songs, see Lester Ruth, "How 'Pop' Are the New Worship Songs? Investigating the Levels of Popular Cultural Influence on Contemporary Worship Music." *Global Forum on Arts and Christian Faith* 3, no. 1 (2015), accessed October 11, 2016, http://www.artsandchristianfaith.org/index.php/journal/article/view/20/19.

21. For a succinct explanation, read John Moxey, "A Guide to Song Forms—Song Form Overview," in *Songstuff*, accessed September 30, 2016, http://www.songstuff.com/song-writing/article/song-form-overview/; for additional reading, consult John Covach, "Form in Rock Music: A Primer," in Walter Everett, *The Foundations of Rock: From "Blue Suede Shoes" to "Suite: Judy Blue Eyes"* (New York: Oxford University Press, 2009).

The aesthetic impact and power of a musical performance lies in its capacity to intensify the attention of the listeners and their consciousness of the present moment by de-automatizing their relationship to the music: a performance at its best breaks down the automatized response that familiar pieces of music invite.[22]

Thus the use of a bridge in "How Great is Our God" served as a transition between the verses and chorus. This musical device provides the possibility of shifting musical direction either toward the verse or the chorus at the inspirational discretion of the worship song leader. Essentially, the use of musical devices like bridge, prechorus, segue, and others alleviates the effect of repetition in contemporary worship songs. While repetition's purpose in these songs helps to create and assert familiarity, repetition could also bear the unintended outcome of being monotonous and automatized. That danger increased when verse and chorus maintained an identical musical structure of harmonic progression and measure count. That repetition of harmonic progression and measure count frequently happened in the verse-chorus-verse-chorus form of many early contemporary worship songs. Again contemporary worship music was following the lead of popular forms of secular music in that popular music had moved to more complex structures in the 1970s and 1980s.[23]

SPANISH-SPEAKING AMERICAN DEVELOPMENTS

At the end of the twentieth century similar changes were occurring in the music of Spanish-speaking contemporary worship congregations. Marcos Witt, little known within the English-speaking contemporary worship community but widely prominent in the Spanish-speaking contemporary worship scene, helped spearhead these developments. Born in Texas and raised in Durango, Mexico, Witt has recorded thirty-two albums, winning five Latin Grammy and two Billboard Awards. Witt's company, CanZion Group, founded in 1987, is reputedly the "largest recording company and distributor for Spanish Christian contemporary music in the world."[24] In 2002, Witt

---

22. Mine Dogantan-Dack, "Familiarity and Musical Performance," in *Music and Famil iarity: Listening, Musicology and Performance,* ed. Elaine King and Helen M. Prior (London: Ashgate Publishing, 2013), 286.

23. Jason Summach, "Form in Top-20 Rock Music, 1955-89," PhD diss., Yale University, 2012, 322.

24. Marcos Witt website, accessed September 30, 2016, http://marcoswitt.net/.

established the Hispanic ministry, Iglesia Lakewood, within Lakewood Church, a Pentecostal church in Houston, and led worship there for ten years. In his musical career, he has collaborated with Hosanna! Music, Maranatha! Music, and mostly recently with Hillsong Music for the latter's *Global Project* (2012).

Witt's songwriting career has spanned the period in which major changes were occurring in contemporary worship music generally: the end of the twentieth and the beginning of the twenty-first centuries. Some of Witt's songs, for example, reflected the older, simpler verse-chorus form like "Renuevame," a 1990 song included in his 2002 album, *El Encuentro.*

In this early writing period of Witt, the melody is based on the primary chords of I – IV – V with a couple instances of relative minor tonalities usage akin to the early days of the contemporary worship song genre. There was no usage of secondary dominants or chromatic mediants in its harmonic organization. The song's rhythm underpinning was kept simple and its rendition ballad-like centering on its devotionally oriented text in an intimate ambience in the same vein as Martin J. Nystrom's "As the Deer" song crafted in 1984.[25]

But structural form does not tell the whole story. In audio samples of this song from 1994 to 2011, there is a discernible difference in the manner in which the song was rendered. The more recent versions showcased its Latin American musical roots.

Witt's work could also reflect the similar exploration of new musical styles found in Anglo songwriters. For example, his song entitled "Alabemos" from 2014 used Electronic Dance Music (EDM) grooves not unlike that found in Chris Tomlin's 2013 song, "God's Great Dance Floor."[26]

ASIAN AND AFRICAN AMERICAN DEVELOPMENTS

The 1990s also witnessed the rise of the contemporary worship music making in the Asian American community. More often than not, these efforts

---

25. Words and music by Marcos Witt, © 1990 Grupo CanZion, admin. by CanZion Group LP. All rights reserved. Used by permission. Audio samples, 1994 version, accessed September 30, 2016, https://youtu.be/xVk0zxwsgLI, 2011 version, https://youtu.be/SNHt wDiRI50.

26. "Alabemos" was composed by Francisco Rene Sotomayor, Jonathan Mark Witt, and Sergio Gonzalez; it was found on the album, *Sigues Siendo Dios.* Sample audio of EDM Mix accessed February 9, 2017, https://www.youtube.com/watch?v=iZnIR9XRdQk&feature=you tu.be. Tomlin's "God's Great Dance Floor" was from his 2013 album, *Passion: Let the Future Begin.* A video sample was accessed on September 30, 2016, https://youtu.be/R-WOneEXr00.

were exclusively known within the Asian diasporic communities given their distinct languages. Previously these communities had been dependent on musical resources that came from their homeland or resorting to ad hoc translation of English contemporary worship songs. For the Chinese-speaking community, this dependency changed when Chinese contemporary worship music entities were established. Unlike other ethnic groups, the Asian effort centered less on any given leading personality, unlike the development of big-name songwriters and worship leaders in the late 1990s among white and black churches and music companies. In contrast, the initial Asian efforts focused on the intent of gifting the minority community with new worship songs, not unlike the earlier impulses of the 1970s. These organizations have shared some of the basic assumptions about the role of music found more broadly across contemporary worship, seeing it as a way of "ushering people into the presence of God through music."[27] (See the discussion of sacramentality in chapter 8.) Of these efforts, 讚美之泉 (Streams of Praise Music Ministries), a California-based outfit established in 1993, has been impressive in its reach beyond the local communities. It has impacted China in both the Three Self Patriotic Movement (government sanctioned) and House Church Movement as well as through Chinese-speaking communities in other parts of the world with their music making.[28]

By and large, the musical practice of an American, English-speaking contemporary worship service situated in an ethnic Chinese congregation tends to lean toward a worship pattern that blends worship styles. It thus might have songs in both English and Chinese (specifically it could be Cantonese, Taiwanese, or Mandarin). In essence, the selected contemporary worship songs are interposed onto a traditional worship service that was formerly hymn based. Often times, this segment of contemporary songs is led by young adults and is inserted just after the segment of Call to Worship consisting of a litany of praise that ends with the Opening Hymn. Typically, this segment would last fifteen to twenty minutes before the pastor comes forward to pray the pastoral prayer. At times this is called the Opening Prayer. Thereafter the traditional service continues. Here is an example of this type of contemporary worship service:[29]

---

27.   Melody of My Heart website accessed September 30, 2016, http://momh.org/; New Heart Music Ministries website accessed September 30, 2016, https://www.newheartmusic .org/t/Main.

28.   Stream of Praise Music Ministries website accessed September 30, 2016, https://www .sop.org/en/about-en/.

29.   See also the worship service of First Chinese Baptist Church, Virginia Beach, VA, accessed September 30, 2016, http://www.fcbc-va.org/bulletin.pdf.

Prelude

(*solemn music, usually a hymn played using a digital organ*)

CALL TO WORSHIP

Invocation

(*Congregation sings "The Lord Is in His Holy Temple"*)[30]

Litany: Psalm 100

(*Responsorially read by the worship leader and the congregation, seated*)

Praise and Worship

(*Featuring an assortment of instruments, e.g., violins, flute, acoustic guitar, and piano with singing of translated English contemporary worship songs from the 1990s–2000s by the congregation that is usually standing, or original Chinese contemporary worship songs from Streams of Praise Music Ministries. Select young adults serve as the worship team.*)

Opening Prayer

(*Soliloquy prayer said by the pastor or an assigned person of the congregation. The people are seated.*)

Hymn of Preparation

Sermon

Closing Hymn

Greetings and Announcement

Offering

Doxology

Benediction

(*The congregation stands, thereafter they sing the Three-Fold Amen before sitting down for a brief time of quiet meditation before leaving the worship space.*)[31]

Meditation

---

30. See example 1.

31. See example 2.

Example 1: "The Lord's is in His Holy Temple." Public Domain.

Example 2: "Three-Fold Amen." Public Domain.

In the African American sector from the 1990s to the present, the contemporary worship music making continues to draw from its gospel roots albeit in new and innovative ways. Some of the more prominent African American artists in that vein include Cece Winans, Yolanda Adams, Byron Cage, Fred Hammond, Israel Houghton, Donnie McClurkin, Bishop Hezekiah Walker, and Kirk Franklin. Among these luminaries, Franklin has significantly pushed the boundary of contemporary worship song in his adoption of "secular" hip-hop and rap as the vehicle of expression.

In a recent National Public Radio interview Franklin discussed his approach to contemporary worship songwriting. In it he reflected standard categories found across contemporary worship, for instance the notion that worship songs can either be vertical (directed to God in prayer) or horizontal (speaking about God to other worshippers). Franklin was quite aware that, in the history of contemporary worship songs, including gospel songs among African American churches, the normal emphasis fell on vertical songs of direct praise to God. (See the discussion of prayer in chapter 6.)

But Franklin also commented on the tension within these songs: by being so vertical they could lose touch with the very "fabric of people's everyday life." Seeing his mission as creating a vision of a "horizontal Jesus," Franklin has sought to write songs relevant to the actual places and struggles found in people's lives:

> Real people live with being Christians with cancer, Christians with AIDS, Christians coming back home with limbs missing from war, Christians being evicted and Christians losing their homes. If you don't paint that picture, too, then I think that you are misrepresenting what the faith really can look like. The faith is not always sunny days. If we don't do that, then I think that we are selling the wrong message."[32]

This particular direction in his music making brings a new perspective to contemporary worship music, which has often been regarded as theologically lightweight. The critique is not entirely without basis in the broad history of contemporary worship music, but Franklin serves as an example that the critique is wrong when the songwriters of contemporary worship have been attentive to one of this liturgical phenomenon's core qualities, namely,

---

32. National Public Radio, "Gospel Star Kirk Franklin Wants to Help You Lose Your Religion," in *All Things Considered* (January 31, 2016), accessed September 30, 2016, http://www.npr.org/2016/01/31/464562711/gospel-star-kirk-franklin-wants-to-help-you-lose-your-religion.

a concern for relevance to contemporary concerns and issues in the lives of worshippers.

While we have highlighted the contribution of Franklin in his use of rap and hip-hop, the lived experience of most African American congregations remains tied to gospel music making with the choir being the centerpiece of its worship life supported by the organ, amply reinforced by additional keyboard, electric guitar, bass guitar, and drums. Thus there is a porousness in any dividing line between worship styles in African American congregations. Those who do contemporary worship tend to bring some element of gospel music making into how they approach contemporary songs.

THE POSSIBLE FUTURE OF CONTEMPORARY WORSHIP MUSIC

So what does the future of contemporary worship music making look like? In surveying the current scene, we see music publishing companies such as Maranatha! Music and Hosanna! Music together with Bethel Music Conference, National Worship Leader Conference, Passion Conference, Worship Together Conference, and others continue to be important channels for music making. Since the 2000s commercial entities such as Capitol Christian Music Group (Capitol CMG) have facilitated the production and distribution of new contemporary worship songs through its stable of artists including Chris Tomlin, Matt Redman, Cece Winans, and Hillsong United among others. Aside from finding these songs online, worship conferences is another platform where these new songs will be shared.

Yet, there is also a discernible shift away from the bright lights of studio and conference to the more intimate setting of a "family room," where the worship space is modeled like a family room filled with the assortment of movable chairs or couches in a circle rather than fixed pews or cinema seats facing toward the front. An example of this is the worship band United Pursuit, a new musical entity based in Knoxville, Tennessee, that is offering an intimate acoustic approach in its music making using this particular type of worship space. It remains to be seen if this effort is viable given its rapid growth through the 1990s Emerging Church movement. Also on the margin in the contemporary music scene are the artists who seek to return hymns to congregational singing in contemporary services. They seek that goal through retexting and retuning strategies. These processes of retexting and retuning refer to the effort of updating the language of old hymns and the matching of new tunes to these hymn texts. Indelible Grace and Cardiphonia are two examples of this movement that seeks to offer contemporary idiomatic expression to hymn texts.

A 1971 "Rock Service" at Arlington Heights United Methodist Church, Fort Worth, Texas.

Source: Courtesy of *Fort Worth Star-Telegram* Collection, Special Collections, The University of Texas at Arlington Libraries, Arlington, Texas. Used by permission.

A sight soon to be very familiar: hands being raised in worship as seen in Jesus People of the early 1970s.

Source: Both images courtesy of KQED-TV, San Francisco as found in Ronald M. Enroth et al., *The Jesus People: Old-Time Religion in the Age of Aquarius* (Grand Rapids: Wm. B. Eerdmans Publishing Co., 1972), 9 and 163. Used by permission.

The staff of Maranatha! Music in 1977.

Source: Chuck Fromm, personal photograph. Used by permission.

Worship at a campus ministry, 1982 (The Wesley Foundation at Stephen F. Austin State University, Nacogdoches, Texas).

Source: Courtesy of the Stephen F. Austin State University Wesley Foundation, Nacogdoches, Texas. Used by permission.

The Anaheim Vineyard Fellowship (originally the Calvary Chapel of Yorba Linda, California) worshipping in a high school gym, ca. 1981.

Source: Walter Reed, personal photograph. Used by permission.

WORSHIP TIMES

THE NEWSLETTER FOR THE CREATIVE WORSHIP LEADER

Volume 1, No.1   A MARANATHA! MUSIC PUBLICATION   WINTER 1986

"Tune My Heart to Sing Thy Praise"

ARE THE NEW SONGS ON KEY?

By Tommy Coomes

Dear God,
I went to your house today. I liked it alot. But I wanted to ask you a question. Do you ever write any new songs?
Love, Susie

Susie's letter raises questions many people are asking. Should Christians create new songs? Is the church willing to worship God using today's music? Do songs have to be old to qualify as sacred?

Missionaries know that people respond best to the Gospel when it is presented in the Language they understand best. The same is true with music. Yet many churches seem to be saying to young people, "We want you to receive Jesus and come to church. But in our worship service you will listen to our kind of music."

Unfortunately, traditional church music just doesn't speak to most young people in the same way it speaks to older church members who have lived with it all their lives.

Like every generation, my generation has a unique personality - especially when it comes to our relationship to music. As teenagers we older baby boomers began an enduring love affair with a new style of music that spoke to our restless, independent spirits.

And rock 'n' roll is here to stay. We are infatuated with the music of our past. The success of motion pictures like *American Graffiti*, TV shows like "Happy Days," and radio stations that play the "oldies but goodies" from the '50s, '60s, and early '70s

proves our fascination with the culture and music we created. Younger boomers are just as attached to their own brand of rock. We can't leave our music behind - and we don't want to leave it outside when we go to church.

Some people claim rock 'n' roll is the music of rebellion. To us, music is just a means of expression. It can express love or hate, good or evil. It depends on the lyrics and the attitude of our hearts.

If music were just a small part of our lives, the tension between church music and contemporary music wouldn't be much of an issue. But the need for music is rooted deep in the human heart.

Music is everywhere. (If not, we take it with us.) It's in our cars, homes, stores, offices, and airports. It even keeps us company on the telephone when we are "on hold". We don't always notice it's there, but music is very powerful.

Music moves the human emotions. Young people usually prefer music that is loud and energetic. As we mature it seems we look for music that provides quiet relief from the stress and strain of life. But the music of the heart always will be the music that meant the most to us during our formative years.

One of the greatest songwriters that ever lived was a young harp player who tended his father's sheep. David was a skilled musician and was in touch with his feelings and his God.

David spoke in a way that others could understand. He pulled feelings out of his soul and wrote them with disarming honesty. His words are still alive, but his melody is lost forever. Maybe that's best. The music that worked so well for David probably wouldn't be accepted in church today, and it would be a shame to lose his powerful message just because we didn't like his melody.

David's understanding of the power of music is reflected in the songs he
(Continued on next page)

Front page of the first issue of *Worship Times* magazine (the predecessor to *Worship Leader* magazine), 1986.

Source: Chuck Fromm. Used by permission.

Cover of Bob Sorge's 1987 book, *Exploring Worship.*

Source: Scanned from the original. Courtesy of Bob Sorge. Used by permission.

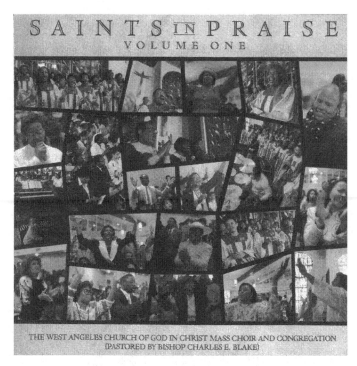

Cover of the West Angeles Church of God in Christ *Saints in Praise* CD, 1989.

Source: *Saints in Praise Vol. One,* West Angeles Church of God in Christ Mass Choir and Congregation, courtesy of Sparrow Records. Used by permission.

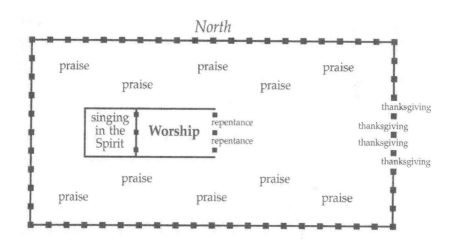

Tabernacle model for constructing a worship set, 1993.

Source: Courtesy of Ruth Ann Ashton. Image found in *God's Presence through Music* (South Bend, IN: LeSEA Publishing, 1993). Used by permission.

CIRCUIT RIDER

For United Methodist Clergy from The United Methodist Publishing House / December / January 1995

Worship

Choices
Conflict
Change

Front cover of theme issue of United Methodist clergy magazine, 1994.

Source: Scanned from the original. *Circuit Rider*, "Worship: Choices, Conflict, Change" (Nashville: United Methodist Publishing House, December 1994–January 1995). Used by permission.

Advertisement used by early United Methodist adopter of contemporary worship in Oneonta, Alabama, early 1990s.

Source: "The Pastor Wears Tennis Shoes," *Circuit Rider* 18, no. 10 (Nashville: United Methodist Publishing House, December 1994/January 1985): 14. Used by permission.

Cover of the first how-to guide on contemporary worship published by Abingdon Press, 1995.

Source: Scanned from the original. Cathy Townley and Mike Graham, *Come Celebrate! A Guide for Planning Contemporary Worship* (Nashville: Abingdon Press, 1995). Used by permission.

Cover of Hosanna! Music cassette tape, 1994.

Source: *Revive Us Again* with Alvin Slaughter
© 1994 Integrity Music, part of the David C Cook family
All rights reserved. Used by permission.

An early adopting Lutheran Church in Houston Texas (Covenant ELCA) worshipping with an overhead projector, 1996.

Source: Kerry Nelson, personal photograph. Used by permission.

Worship at Iglesia Metodista Unida San Marcos (a Spanish-speaking United Methodist Church) in Baytown, Texas, 2005.

Source: Silverio Sanchez Sr., personal photograph. Used by permission.

IMAG (image magnification), lighting, and haze machine, Passion City Church, Atlanta, Georgia, 2016.

Source: Courtesy of Passion City Church. Photo credit: Allie Hine (top) and Roxy Moure (bottom). Used by permission.

A production room in use.

Source: Courtesy of Phil Bowdle, Creative Arts pastor, West Ridge Church, Dallas, GA. Used by permission.

A video switcher used to select images for projection.

Source: Image courtesy of Luke Flowers, Technical Director of First Assembly Community Ministries, Lafayette, IN. Used by permission.

Examples of environmental projection.

Source: Courtesy of Stephen Proctor, http://www.illuminate.us. Used by permission.

Chapter 6
PRAYER AND CONTEMPORARY WORSHIP

Imagine three worshippers praying.

Worshipper 1 pours out her prayer. Convinced that nothing can separate us from the love of God, she cries, "Thank you, Jesus. Oh, thank you, thank you, Jesus. Yes. Oh, my heart is overwhelmed. Thank you, Jesus." After repeatedly expressing her gratitude, the worshipper concludes her prayer: "Oh, my heart is overflowing with joy, with joy, with joy, with joy for you, Jesus, for you, Jesus."

Worshipper 2 is likewise caught up in awe of the Lord in an exhilarating feeling that the provision of God is greater than any of life's obstacles. This worshipper's prayer is a simple affirming of the reliability of divine goodness: "Yes, Lord; Yes, Lord; Yes, yes, Lord." Time and again the worshipper repeats this loop, lost in wonder, love, and praise.

Worshipper 3 is abounding in a newfound knowledge of God's forgiveness. Having felt the power of God from heaven as a rushing mighty wind, the worshipper prays, first whispering and then shouting, "Adoration to God and the Lamb!...Glory to God! Glory and adoration to God and the Lamb forever!" Over and over he praises God.

These examples show the importance of prayer in contemporary worship. A recurring quality of this worship style has been to speak honestly and authentically with God. Whether in the teaching that worship should have a vertical, human-to-God dimension—and not just a horizontal, person-to-person dimension—to be true worship or in the experience of having spiritual encounters when singing to God and not just about God, contemporary worship has valued praying.

The examples also show the importance of praying extemporaneously. Usually in contemporary worship, the prayer has been spontaneously composed. Except when a Bible passage is being used or in those mainline congregations that might mingle in a written prayer, contemporary worshippers pray extemporaneously, especially in the midst of heightened emotions as in these examples.

Finally, the three examples also reveal that prayer practices in contemporary worship are not entirely new, but belong to long trajectories in non-text-based worship traditions. Some aspects of contemporary worship are not that contemporary, and that includes many dimensions of prayer. We slipped in a little sleight of hand to make this point. Although the first two examples come from the recent contemporary worship world (example 1 is an impromptu prayer by Kim Walker-Smith, a Jesus Culture worship leader from Bethel Church in Redding, California, and example 2 is a fictitious worshipper singing the chorus from Darrell Evans's 1998 song "Trading My Sorrows"), the last comes from the account of the conversion of an early Methodist songwriter, John Adam Granade, over two hundred years ago.[1] Yet at first glance all three appear to be coming from the same worlds of worship. Corporate prayer in contemporary worship continues traits from earlier non-text-based worship, which unfortunately have been little studied in either their past or present forms.

This chapter thus will generally describe the prayer of contemporary worship. We will not offer a strict chronological account although we will note (when we can) significant developments in the praying of this style of worship, beginning with the move to updated English in the first surge of contemporary worship in the 1960s. We also will not offer a history of daily public prayer (the "office"), which is a standard topic of books on the broad history of Christian worship because that liturgical form is not important within contemporary worship.

PRAYER AND CONTEMPORARY WORSHIP'S DEFINING QUALITIES

A change in the language by which English-speaking Christians spoke to God in corporate worship was a significant liturgical development in the second half of the twentieth century. The change was foundational: to move from archaic to updated English was considered the essence of making worship contemporary in the 1960s. To lose *thee, thou,* and *thy* as the way to talk

---

1. Walker-Smith's prayer comes at the end of the song "Unstoppable Love" on the *This Is Jesus Culture* CD (Jesus Culture Music, 2015); Granade's conversion account is from R. N. Price, *Holston Methodism: From Its Origin to the Present Time* (Nashville: Publishing House of the Methodist Episcopal Church, South, 1912), 2:7–8.

to God was the first domino to fall on the path to today. To believe that we pray best to God in contemporary language is now a universal presumption of contemporary worship and one of its defining qualities. It is so much assumed and caught on so quickly, in fact, that most people would now point to other qualities like music or technology as the features that make worship contemporary. (The change was also expansive: eliminating archaic English spread across all Protestant and Roman Catholic worship, but that's a different story.)

But in the 1960s, using contemporary language wasn't just assumed; it had to be defended and celebrated as appropriate. For example, at the dawn of the 1970s, liturgical historian James White—himself then a worship experimenter—argued that merely substituting new words for old did not go far enough. A shift in contemporary people's worldview meant that it was no longer appropriate to approach God through the language etiquette of royal rituals. For White, "ancient forms of reverential address in prayers" were so out of sync with modern people that they were inauthentic.[2]

Since many shared White's opinion, changes in prayer language happened quickly. Whether in extemporaneous prayers, written prayers, or songs that were prayers, a massive shift occurred from the late 1960s to the early 1980s. If you listen to recordings of extemporaneous prayer over that time span, you will notice it occurring. A review of the collections of newly written, contemporary prayers reveals the same shift. And after the mid-1980s, all of the top contemporary worship songs that achieved widespread popularity were written in the same updated English of the new Bible translations that their composers read devotionally.

The shift in the language of new Bible versions and the shift in prayer language are intertwined. As contemporary worshippers of the 1960s and 1970s began to read new versions like Today's English Version (notice the name) they changed how they prayed and sang. Indeed, using a Bible like the King James Version that has archaic language seems necessary to maintain the perception that talking to God requires a distinctive language, and to maintain the capacity to extemporize correctly in English that one doesn't normally use.

The link between updated Bibles and prayer shows, too, the direction of the changes in language toward a greater colloquialism. The turn toward colloquial speech, heard as truer and more authentic, has been a larger cultural shift since the 1960s. This attraction to the colloquial in prayer gets expressed

---

2. James F. White, *New Forms of Worship* (New York, Nashville: Abingdon Press, 1971), 198–202.

in several ways in contemporary worship. Pray-ers should speak to God as if speaking to a friend or should pray with the honesty and expressiveness of a child since "prayer is simply talking to God," as expressed by one contemporary worship designer.[3]

The turn toward colloquial speech in praying has gone hand in hand with making prayer accessible to people and relevant to their concerns, other defining qualities for contemporary worship. Various means have developed to achieve those goals like the sharing of joys and concerns or creating teams to pray with worshippers at the end of a service, although neither are universal practices.

To mention this latter practice, often called ministry time, highlights the different venues for prayer in contemporary worship. Prayer within contemporary worship occurs in several outlets. Two are related to the extended time of congregational singing known as the worship set. The songs themselves are the primary outlet for prayer in a contemporary service. The second is the praying that takes place around the songs to help provide a seamless flow through the set or provide transition into or out of singing.

The third outlet involves the praying that takes place outside the worship set but within the service. Often this prayer is connected with the reading and preaching of scripture. Or it could occur in activities like ministry time.

A final outlet involves prayer in the broader life of congregations that supplements the prayer within services as well as prepares for worship. This prayer can be both corporate and individual. How contemporary worshippers pray in all four outlets will be considered in turn.

PRAYING, SINGING, AND WORSHIP SETS

Holland Davis, longtime Calvary Chapel worship leader and pastor, expresses a central sentiment and common practice of contemporary worship: "Corporate worship is prayer set to music."[4] Sung prayer, a historic staple of Christian worship, reaches new heights in contemporary worship's song sets. In a typical service the songs themselves carry much of the weight for speaking to God in prayer.

---

3. Kim Miller, *[Re]designing Worship: Creating Powerful God Experiences* (Nashville: Abingdon Press, 2009), 103. Anthropologist T. M. Luhrmann notes the same in *When God Talks Back: Understanding the American Evangelical Relationship with God* (New York: Alfred A. Knopf, 2012), 47.

4. Holland Davis, *Let It Rise: A Manual for Worship* (Alachua: Bridge-Logos, 2009), 2.

Worshippers today should thank contemporary worship's Pentecostal origins for songs having that importance. Although not the only source for contemporary worship, important Pentecostal developments of the mid-twentieth century, spilling over to other traditions through charismatic renewal movements, established praise as a key to corporate prayer engagement with God. In the Pentecostal revival of the 1940s and 1950s known as the Latter Rain Movement, for example, preachers lifted up praise as *the* critical part of worship. (See chapter 8.) Although this revival's corporate expressions of praise could take many forms—spoken, shouted, or singing in the Spirit (i.e., harmonious singing in tongues or in individually composed short statements)—songs that praised God became an important fixture. Not surprisingly, one of the early names for the new songs that have characterized contemporary worship was *praise chorus*, a name that had a surge in published use from the mid-1980s.

In the 1970s and 1980s, which is the formative period for firming up contemporary worship's ongoing sensibilities and practices, ways of linking praise's priority to an emphasis upon sung prayer emerged. One was to speak of the value of singing *to* God, not just *about* God, an early emphasis of John Wimber, Carl Tuttle, and others associated with the important Anaheim Vineyard congregation.[5] This emphasis was not and has not remained only a sensibility of Vineyard churches, however. Distinguishing between singing to God and about God can be found more broadly, too.

For some the surge in songs *to* God was itself a gift *from* God. For Pentecostal author LaMar Boschman, for example, the increase in the number of songs singing to the Lord was God's doing in the late 1970s. Previously he remembers songs that mainly spoke about God. According to this popular teacher, "[there was in the late 1970s] an influx of songs that caused the believer to sing *to* the Lord instead of *about* Him. They helped to direct our hearts in vertical worship—not just horizontal communication."[6]

This distinguishing between vertical and horizontal worship—between worship content directed to God and content where people spoke to each other—is the second way of linking praise's priority to an emphasis upon sung prayer. According to Kent Henry, another well-traveled Pentecostal teacher, having churches pay less attention to "horizontal songs" and more

---

5. Andy Park, Lester Ruth, and Cindy Rethmeier, *Worshiping with the Anaheim Vineyard: The Emergence of Contemporary Worship* (Grand Rapids: Wm. B. Eerdmans Publishing Co., 2017).

6. LaMar Boschman, *A Heart of Worship: Experience a Rebirth of Worship* (Lake Mary: Creation House, 1994), 111.

to "vertical songs" was an important development he saw in churches that moved to praise and worship (contemporary) services in the mid-1980s.[7]

Of course, a developing distinction between praise and worship that teachers were making sometimes meant that *praise* was more associated with horizontal worship (as the songs praised God's attributes and activity) and *worship* with vertical worship (as the songs spoke directly to God about the worshipper's relationship with God). Although a common distinction, it was not a universal one, and other authors recognized that in practice it was an artificial one. Regardless, the net result was to establish a widespread sensibility in the 1980s that worship sets ought to move toward songs that prayerfully spoke to God, whether one wanted to call that praise, worship, or adoration. Consequently, it is not surprising that songs such as "I Love You, Lord," "As the Deer," and "I Exalt Thee" enjoyed long runs as popular songs, as top-25 song lists began to emerge from CCLI in 1989. The songs' prayerfulness—and suitability for the end of a song set—were reinforced by the sound of their music.

Beyond the popularity of such songs, there are other evidences of an innate sensibility in contemporary worship to pray while singing. One evidence is having names for music companies that themselves are prayers (Maranatha! Music or ThankYou Music). Another indication is songwriters appending new choruses that pray to God to the lyrics of older hymns that were not prayers. But the strongest evidence of a sense of the essential propriety to pray while singing is the overwhelming tendency for the most popular contemporary worship songs to contain prayer. It is a tendency that has only increased over the years. It was common for songs in songbooks in the early 1970s to not be prayers. For example, less than one-third of the songs in Campus Crusade for Christ's *Pass It On* (1972), the Maranatha Evangelical Association's (an arm of the important Calvary Chapel in Costa Mesa, California) *Rejoice in Jesus Always* (1973), and United Methodism's *Ventures in Song* (1972) were prayers. Not surprisingly, of the thirty-eight songs that have ever appeared on a CCLI top-25 list for the United States from 1989 to early 2016 and are *not* prayers, twenty-nine were written in 1989 or before. Indeed, only one-third, that is, ten songs, of all top songs with copyright dates of 1979 or before (thirty songs) have been prayers. In contrast, 85 percent of the top songs with copyright dates of 1990 or later have included prayer. The tendency for the most popular songs to be prayers has been persistent, becoming even more likely as time goes by.

---

7. Kent Henry, "Worship's Current Phases & Future Trends," *The Psalmist Magazine* (April/May 1988): 5.

Even as the most popular songs have grown in the likelihood of being prayers, what have worshippers been praying when they have sung these songs? Of course, the actual practice in any one contemporary service might be different as other songs and spoken prayers are used, but tendencies in these top CCLI songs show clear prayer trends, especially when cross-checked against other collections of songs over the decades. To determine these tendencies in prayer for this book, we examined the 114 songs on CCLI's top-25 lists from 1989 to February 2016 for types of prayer, comparing them against more than a dozen other collections from the early 1970s to early 2000s. Several trends emerge in the prayer content of the top songs:

- Songs that honored God in thanks, praise, adoration, or in affirming positive attributes or actions about God have always had a dominant presence among the top songs.

- There has been a shift, however, in how the top songs honor God. Direct statements of praise and adoration (think phrases like "I lift and praise your name" or "Lord, I love you") have given way since the mid-2000s to more of a tendency to generally affirm positive attributes or actions about God (think "You, our God, are mighty and powerful, the creator of the world").

- This shift in honoring is a relative, not absolute, shift in weight of emphasis since recent songs still contain some direct expressions of praise and adoration.

- If a song requests something from God, the request is overwhelmingly likely to be self-directed, seeking something for those worshippers or invoking divine presence.

- In these top songs, there is almost no intercession for others.

- Songs that explore in prayer the relationship between God and the worshipper speak about this relationship in multiple ways, including desiring God (a particularly popular idiom in the 1980s and 1990s), but there is very little confession of sin, failure, or fault and absolutely no laments of complaints or distress with God.

- The complexity of prayer within a single song has been increasing over the years in that recently written songs are likely to contain more prayer and more kinds of prayer sentiments in a single song.

95

- The top songs tend to pray to God, the Lord, or Jesus (or Jesus as God or Lord), not explicitly to God the Father or the Holy Spirit. Most songs want to love on Jesus.

Of course, these are only conclusions about tendencies of the top songs considered outside of an actual service. In any contemporary service, past or present, there are other songs as well as spoken prayers. The actual praying in a service can be broader. Let's consider these other outlets for prayer in contemporary worship.

PRAYING IN THE SETS BEYOND THE SONGS

Although the primary means of praying in a contemporary service, the songs themselves are not the only prayers. Usually the worship set will contain prayers—either spoken or semi-sung in a kind of heightened speech—located in and around the songs. Such praying, especially when done well, helps provide a seamless flow through the set and heightens the sense of actual engagement of the congregation with God. More times than not the worship leader, the main musician, will handle these prayers. Having a musician with this responsibility in the initial part of a service is a way of showing the centrality of musicians in liturgical leadership, which is another of the defining qualities of contemporary worship.

The term *worship leader* and the development of this role in the early 1980s[8] suggest the propriety of having musicians pray and not only the pastor or preacher. Evolving from earlier terms like *song leader* or *music director*, the term "*worship* leader" is linked to the sense of worship, which was developing in the 1970s and 1980s, where worship was direct vertical interaction with and to the Lord, especially in prayer. A song leader just helped a congregation sing a song; a worship leader facilitated worshippers' meeting with God. Praying seems a natural responsibility in such encounters.

Interestingly, until recently, there appears to have been little attention given to addressing worship leaders' capacity to pray well. Neither the educational materials from early worship conferences nor the growing number of books on being a worship leader from the mid-1980s forward speak much

---

8. See Nelson Cowan, "Lay-Prophet-Priest: The Not-So Fledgling 'Office' of the Worship Leader," *Liturgy* 32, 1 (2017): 24–31 for a short history of this term's development and the responsibilities of the position.

about how to lead in corporate prayer. Attention to individual formation in private prayer is a more frequent topic. This omission suggests that worship leaders learned how to pray by watching others pray; it suggests, too, that long-standing aspects of extemporaneous evangelical praying were likely to be continued.

Despite the lack of educational materials for early worship leaders, musicians grasped their role as pray-ers. The actual dynamics when leading worship reinforced the propriety, even necessity, of their praying. One early worship leader, for instance, still remembers the reasons why he prayed: proximity to the microphone, the desire to avoid dead time in order to have a seamless flow in the set and "maintain the moment," and his knowledge of where the service was going, he having had a major creative hand in shaping it.[9] His experience seems typical. Since pastors or preachers are rarely on stage during the set, waiting on them to come forward to pray creates dead time, breaking the flow. Nonetheless some churches, like the Lutheran megachurch Community Church of Joy, still relied upon the preachers to be the main pray-ers.[10]

Recent efforts have sought to overcome the lack of early instructional materials to help musicians handle corporate praying (to be fair, the topic is not stressed in the training of pastors either). There is a growing awareness, as worship leader Zac Hicks has recently stated, that the changing roles between preachers and musicians means "that worship leaders are the main facilitators of the Church's corporate prayer encounter with God."[11]

Therefore recent coaches of worship leaders have sought to step into that gap and provide instruction as to how to pray well within a worship set. For instance, Paul Baloche, in a 2003 DVD on creating flow, instructs other musicians how to plan for prayers within a set.[12] Particularly useful is his advocacy for internalizing the Psalms, praying them repeatedly in the worship space, to be able to draw upon this language naturally in worship. His modeling on the DVD shows an integration of psalm verses, phrases from song lyrics, and standard phrases from evangelical piety. His prayers invite worshippers into

---

9. Douglas Anthony, interview by Lester Ruth, September 10, 2015.

10. Timothy Wright, interview by Lester Ruth, February 6, 2015.

11. Zac M. Hicks, *The Worship Pastor: A Call to Ministry for Worship Leaders and Teams* (Grand Rapids: Zondervan, 2016), 60.

12. Paul Baloche, *Leading Worship: Creating Flow*, Modern Worship Series (Lindale: Leadworship.com, 2003), DVD. See also Paul Baloche, "Praying during Worship," uploaded December 13, 2007, accessed September 27, 2016, https://www.youtube.com/watch?v=-09zwbj8a2o.

deeper engagement with and appropriation of the song lyrics, personalizing them and adapting them to individual expression.

Common practice is often the opposite of what is being prescribed in teaching materials. Thus instructional materials like Baloche's provide glimpses of typical practices but in a reverse way. Thus, to counter a stronger preference for spontaneity, Rich Muchow, former worship leader at Saddleback Church, affirmed that the Holy Spirit can be active in planning and preparing prayers ahead of a service, not just in extemporaneity.[13] Even more tongue in cheek—but not any less accurately—Jon Nicol encourages worship leaders to avoid the "capo prayer," unthinking filler to buy time for the leader to place the capo on the guitar.[14]

Different strands of contemporary worship can show their own character in how people pray. Pentecostal worship leaders, like the Kim Walker-Smith example from the beginning of the chapter, often show more ecstatic forms of prayer, including prayers that are sung in a kind of heightened speech. In contrast, contemporary services in mainline congregations whose tradition has written prayers may show that influence by using written prayers individually or for congregational use by projection. Common to all contemporary worship, however, is to continue instrumental music underneath the prayers associated with the worship set.

PRAYING ELSEWHERE IN THE SERVICE

While the worship set carries much of the weight for praying, it is not the only time contemporary worshippers speak to God. In a typical service there are other prayers, although the diversity among congregations—and even the fluidity of practice within a single congregation—makes describing universal patterns impossible. Nonetheless, there are tendencies and common practices that recur frequently.

Two common tendencies are for praying to occur as a way of preparing for a new act of worship or concluding one. The former serves to recognize that what follows is an opportunity to engage with God and to request God to make it so. To conclude by prayer offers a chance to respond to encountering

---

13. Rick Muchow, *The Worship Answer Book: More Than a Music Experience* (Nashville: J. Countryman, 2006), 230–31.

14. Jon Nicol, "8 Ways to Avoid the Capo Prayer," accessed September 26, 2016, https://worshipleader.com/leadership/eight-ways-to-avoid-the-capo-prayer/. See also Jon Nicol, *Worship Flow: 28 Ways to Create Great Segues* (FlingWide Publishing, 2016), 61–63, 127–29.

God, or as a means to reinforce in worshippers what had just taken place, as in the case of many prayers offered after sermons.

Given these two sweeping purposes of prayer (preparing and responding), individual prayers within a contemporary service can fall in a multitude of places in the larger order. Different congregations show great variety; a single congregation can plan to pray at different spots in the order of worship from service to service. Across the range of contemporary services, however, praying often occurs toward the beginning of a service, before or after the reading of scripture, before or after the sermon, before or after an offering (if one is taken), during Communion (if administered), and at the conclusion of the service. In Pentecostal forms of contemporary worship, especially early ones, the entire congregation could be swept up in praying individually as well. Regardless of placement, pray-ers typically speak in ways that reflect elements of contemporary worship's ethos since the 1960s: whatever is spoken must be relevant, intelligible, and immediate to that congregation. In other words, like all elements in a contemporary service, worshippers expect prayers to be authentic to them. No single prayer, even the Lord's Prayer, is a strict necessity.

Many churches express an interesting difference between when they are singing prayers (i.e., songs) and when they are speaking them. The difference is, which Person of the Trinity is addressed in prayer? If a specific person of the Godhead is named, songs tend to be more addressed to Jesus Christ and spoken prayers to the Father.

Regardless of whether prayer is addressed to God the Father or to Jesus Christ, it appears there is less spoken prayer in the typical contemporary service as compared to noncontemporary styles of worship. Although no exhaustive study exists, one worship scholar's work suggests the amount of time saying spoken prayers is less in contemporary worship than in liturgical, traditional, or blended services.[15] Particularly striking in contemporary services is the absence of intercessory prayer for others and confession of sin.

In many instances the loss of intercessions for others can be tied to the loss of an all-encompassing pastoral prayer in contemporary worship. This kind of lengthy prayer serves as the main prayer time in many traditional services. In it the pastor prays for parishioners, church, and world by interceding, petitioning, confessing, thanking, or praising as the pastor feels appropriate. In traditional worship, shouldering this prayer is a critical worship-leading

---

15. Constance Cherry, "My House Shall Be Called a House of…Announcements," https://iws.edu/wp-content/uploads/2012/05/Cherry-article-My-House.pdf, accessed October 3, 2016.

responsibility of the pastor. Occasionally a contemporary service will retain a pastoral prayer, perhaps adapted and more interactive. As likely, however, is a jettisoning of a single long prayer, particularly one said by the pastor.

The reasons for the loss of a pastoral prayer are multiple. The logistics of maintaining flow in a service work against retaining it. Not only are pastors not immediately available to step quickly to the front to pray since they are usually seated among the congregation, but a long prayer by a single person violates a sense of flow. The loss of a pastoral prayer is connected, too, to the changing perception about the pastor's role in leading worship. Since the rise of musicians as worship leaders, a pastor is much more likely to be thought of mainly as the preacher or "teaching pastor"—to use a term that has gained favor since the late 1980s—with a limited liturgical role.

Regardless of who is saying the prayer, the tendency is for extemporaneous prayer. Indeed, for many worshippers, the prayers must be composed spontaneously to be considered authentic and spiritual; song lyrics are the only exception to having prewritten prayers. This preference—little studied—is a longstanding one in many strands of Protestant worship, especially evangelical or Free Church ones.

Indeed, because of the similarity in internal dynamics of all evangelical extemporaneous praying, whether past or present, traditional or contemporary, we can expect overlap in how the prayers are composed and even in what they are likely to say. That is the point we were making at this chapter's beginning by including the story of John Adam Granade, the early Methodist. The dynamics for praying extemporaneously are the same. Consequently, contemporary extemporaneous prayers sound much like historic extemporaneous prayers, whether of the remote past like early Methodism or more recent.[16]

Extemporaneous praying is not purely spontaneous. It uses formulas derived from several sources: short biblical allusions or quotes; short allusions or quotes from other liturgical materials like songs; other phrases circulating in a people's spirituality; and short phrases or words that become standard. All are learned by listening to other people pray. Together the formulas form a repertoire from which a pray-er pulls. Some formulas are used for structure to begin and end prayers or to move the prayer along, while others provide the prayer's content. Sometimes pray-ers do not change the formulas from prayer to prayer, or they might adapt them for a particular context. The result

---

16. For a description of recent praying, see Jeff Todd Titon, *Powerhouse for God: Speech, Chant, and Song in an Appalachian Baptist Church* (Austin: University of Texas Press, 1988), 278–88.

is a significant degree of repetition and predictability from prayer to prayer, especially from any single pray-er, and even over time.

Because of the formulaic nature of extemporaneous praying, much of extemporaneous praying does not sound like ordinary conversation with a friend, despite how often this goal is stated in the literature. Use of standard formulas like repeating a divine name at the beginning of sentences, using phrases like "be with," "bless," and "we come to you," and repetition of the word "just" have all become standard features for extemporaneous praying. To these word formulas, we should add certain rhythms of speech, gestures, and tone of voice as common features of extemporaneous praying. Indeed, the formulas and practices are so common that they can be spoofed, either in YouTube clips or new versions of the Lord's Prayer: "Our Father in heaven, we want to come to you this evening hour asking you that your name might be hallowed. And Father, we also want to ask that your kingdom may come. . . ."[17]

As mentioned above, the loss of substantial intercession for the world has occurred frequently. But many congregations have utilized a time of praying that adds a significant degree of petitioning for individual worshippers, usually toward the end of the service. This ministry time or prayer ministry—both frequently used terms—became common in early strands of contemporary worship, especially in Pentecostal churches. It has spread and can be found in mainline congregations, too, perhaps due to charismatic movement influences. It represents another leveling of the roles for worship leading, in that the pray-ers usually are laypeople. Participation is voluntary as people express the need to be prayed for. While the prayer might take place in the main worship space—setting up prayer ministers during the reception of Communion is one variation—taking those who want to be prayed for to a separate space has been common. A ministry time usually occurs toward the end of the service.

CONTEMPORARY CONGREGATIONS AS PRAYING CONGREGATIONS

The larger prayer life of a congregation is the fourth outlet for prayer in contemporary worship. The whole picture of a congregation's prayer activities must be considered to understand its prayer, not just a look at its worship

---

17. "What If We Talked to People Like We Talked to God?," accessed September 26, 2016, https://www.youtube.com/watch?v=xms1uf-bnXs; Laurence Hull Stookey, *Let the Whole Church Say Amen! A Guide for Those Who Pray in Public* (Nashville: Abingdon Press, 2001), 37.

services. For example, some congregations have removed spoken intercessions and petitions from their main services in order to highlight these prayers in their home groups.[18] Look only at their Sunday services and one would overlook this important dimension of their wider prayer activity.

Praying together outside worship services provides an important fabric in congregational life and is an essential backdrop for the services. The opportunities can be numerous, as anthropologist T. M. Luhrmann notes: small groups, prayer walks, or even sharing with another Christian who holds the unofficial office of prayer warrior.[19] Even though the mid-week prayer meeting has been in decline since the mid-twentieth century, no similar decline has occurred in how contemporary worshipping congregations view prayer: it is essential for congregational vitality. Consequently, some congregations delight in the breadth of their broader prayer life as Walt Kallestad, a groundbreaker in early Lutheran contemporary worship, did in 1996, reporting two thousand people a month in his Community Church of Joy involved in various forms of prayer ministry.[20] Twenty-four/seven prayer, in fact, happens in a few congregations both in contemporary worship's past (in the early 1970s at Bethel Tabernacle, a Pentecostal church in Redondo Beach, California)[21] and present (the International House of Prayer in Kansas City, Kansas).

Prayer occurs as a special way to prepare for the main service in many congregations. It is typical for the musicians, pastors, and others involved in the service to gather and pray as a final act of preparation. A few congregations have held regular special services to bathe their entire liturgical life in prayer. Others have designated groups to pray for their worship services. Their practices vary: they meet with the clergy just prior to the service, or they pray for the upcoming service every day, or they walk through the space ahead of time and pray for everything and everyone in the upcoming service, or they are engaged in prayer for the service during the service.

Like other churches, congregations with contemporary services emphasize the development of personal practices of prayer. Such devotional practices especially impact contemporary worship when practiced by the musicians and pastors who lead it, which is why many of the early guides for being

---

18. Hope Chapels are the example. See Ralph Moore, *Let Go of the Ring* (Honolulu: Straight Street Publishing, 1983), 113–14.

19. Luhrmann, *When God Talks Back*, 49–50.

20. Walt Kallestad, *Entertainment Evangelism: Taking the Church Public* (Nashville: Abingdon Press, 1996), 89.

21. Brian Vachon, *A Time to Be Born* (Englewood Cliffs: Prentice-Hall, Inc., 1972), 46.

a worship leader reinforce the necessity to develop individual prayer. These guides remind worship leaders to be in prayer as they are planning services. When practiced faithfully, one worship leader testified, the intertwining of prayer and song selection promotes internalizing the songs, leading to a special quality in the leading of worship.[22] Personal devotions have sparked new songs, too. Many of the available testimonies about the origins of popular songs, particularly older ones, speak of their spontaneously happening while the songwriter was engaged in prayer and Bible reading, musical instrument in hand. "As the Deer," "Lord, Be Glorified," and "Lord, I Lift Your Name on High" are all examples.[23]

Regardless of when, by whom, or how, the literature describing a proper background for contemporary worship uniformly stresses the importance of prayer in a church. Pentecostal author Bob Sorge states this presumption dramatically: "I'm going to tell you why some worship services take so long to get off the ground, or why some don't even fly at all. This is the reason behind every faltering worship service, every time. It is simply this. We have not been living out the word of Scripture that commands, 'Pray without ceasing.'"[24]

---

22.   Stephen R. Phifer, *Worship That Pleases God: The Passion and Reason of True Worship* (Victoria, BC: Trafford Publishing, 2005), 298.

23.   Phil Christensen and Shari MacDonald, *Our God Reigns: The Stories behind Your Favorite Praise and Worship Songs* (Grand Rapids: Kregel Publications, 2000), 17, 109, 113.

24.   Bob Sorge, *In His Face: A Prophetic Call to Renewed Focus* (Kansas City: Oasis House, 1994), 119.

Chapter 7
THE BIBLE AND PREACHING IN CONTEMPORARY WORSHIP

In the beginning was a word, that is, in the beginning of contemporary worship. Although many today would associate contemporary worship with contemporary music, it actually was a concern for the use of contemporary words in worship that lie at the headwaters of this new form of worship. In those early years those who desired a new way of worship expressed that goal by seeking new ways to voice *the* word, the Bible, in worship. Sometimes it was the use of scripture directly appropriated to provide the words for new songs. Or it was in the imaginative creation of new teaching, paying close attention to verses given very little previous consideration, to provide the rationale for new worship paths into the presence of God. And it was in the tsunami of new versions of the Bible starting in the 1960s that sought to express truth in today's English of contemporary people. Along with a related overhaul of the language of prayer at the time, the language—the words—English-speaking worshippers used to hear from and talk to God flipped within a generation. Sometimes the search for a contemporary word has been in the reshaping of preaching, starting with experiments in the 1960s that gained steam in the 1970s.

And, regardless of those dimensions of the word's impact on the beginnings of contemporary worship, today's ubiquitous form of contemporary worship planning starts not with music or the arts but with the word. In congregation after congregation in this developed stage of contemporary worship, the first choices made are scriptural ones: what will be this week's biblical text and what will be the theme derived from it? Making those decisions is the trigger to releasing creative consideration of what music and arts to use as well as a myriad of other choices in service design.

And so, in the beginning of contemporary worship was a word, not a (musical) note. We will proceed in this chapter to look at the critical scriptural dimensions of contemporary worship, tracing their historical connections and impact on this way of worship, beginning with the desire for up-to-date language.

A CONTEMPORARY WORD IN CONTEMPORARY WORDS

Worship historian James F. White in his 1971 book *New Forms of Worship*, which was a defense for contemporary worship of that time, saved discussing the language of worship until his last chapter. This delay wasn't because the issue wasn't important. White's reason was the opposite:

> Most people who talk about new forms of worship think immediately of changes in the words used in worship. They often equate experimentation with the modernizing of the vocabulary of a worship service. If nothing else, this common identification of contemporary worship with updating the language shows us just how verbal our fixation has been.[1]

Although our ears today may have gotten used to updated English in worship, at the start of the 1970s to have heard worship led in contemporary language was striking. It is no wonder the profound nature of the change in language first characterized what the "contemporary" of contemporary worship meant at the time. Indeed, White's book did not even have a chapter on music.

Not only was it conspicuous that *thee*'s and *thou*'s were being changed to colloquial English but the quickness of the liturgical change was remarkable as well. Even as late as 1966, one casual observer, noting he was a "prisoner" of the *wast*s and *dost*s, estimated that 98 percent of Protestant churches still used archaic language on Sunday morning.[2] This tradition would soon change as Protestants across the board—and Roman Catholics, too, if one counts post-Vatican II liturgical reforms—overturned centuries of practice in less than two decades. While the shift was widespread, those churches experimenting in services named "contemporary" emphasized updating language as their cutting edge. Being up-to-date in language was what contemporary worship meant before other defining qualities (see chapter 1) became settled.

---

1. James F. White, *New Forms of Worship* (Nashville: Abingdon Press, 1971), 195.

2. Kenneth L. Wilson, "Help! I'm a Prisoner of the Wasts and Dosts," *Christian Herald* (June 1966): 24.

The move toward today's language affected everyone even though mainline congregations were the ones using the *contemporary worship* term at that time. Evangelicals at the headwaters of the larger phenomenon also pursued everyday English. California street preacher Arthur Blessitt, for example, began his ministry in 1967 using the King James Version of the Bible to preach and worship, but changed when he found out that young people didn't understand it. He shifted to the Today's English Version (the Good News Bible), which the American Bible Society supplied him by the thousands for distribution. He found those affected by his ministry began to pray and sing in more contemporary, colloquial English.[3]

This sort of shift in worship language seems tied to the rise in new Bible translations, although it is hard to tell whether the shift was a result of the new versions as in Blessitt's case. It might be that the simultaneous changes in worship and scripture were parallel signs of a growing cultural preference for more colloquial expression. Regardless, the radicalness of the change in worship language in the late twentieth century has been matched by the volume of new versions of the Bible being published at the same time. One scholar has characterized this scriptural rush as a "flood," estimating that the 1,500 translations of the Bible (in whole or in part, i.e., a single book) from Greek and Hebrew into English from 1526 to 1900 have been matched by the same number of new translations (1,500) from 1900 to the start of the twenty-first century. Much of this flood has come since 1945.[4] Several of the most popular new translations came out in the 1960s and 1970s.

Even if the new Bible versions did not cause churches to experiment in early forms of contemporary worship, several connecting points are still evident. One is the overlap in time. Many of the most popular new translations were published during the initial rise of the term *contemporary worship* from the late 1960s through late 1970s: the Living Bible (New Testament in 1967; whole Bible in 1971); the Good News Bible/Today's English Version (New Testament, 1966; whole, 1976); and the New International Version (New Testament, 1973; whole, 1978). Another connection is the use of these new translations. In contemporary service after service, it was a newer version—not the King James Version—that was read. The latter's archaic English

---

3. Arthur Blessitt, e-mail to Lester Ruth, May 29, 2014.

4. David Daniell, *The Bible in English: Its History and Influence* (New Haven: Yale University Press, 2003), 734, 764, 769. See also Paul D. Wegner, *The Journey from Texts to Translations: The Origin and Development of the Bible* (Grand Rapids: Baker Books, 1999), 394–95.

had even been set aside in the writing of the most popular contemporary worship songs by the mid-1980s.[5]

To connect new Bible translations and the emergence of contemporary worship is reasonable, too, because they all rest upon a common assumption: the Christian message needs to be in a form that is intelligible to contemporary or modern people. Whether in the words of the Bible or the words of worship, scripture translators and contemporary worship leaders presume language needs to be accessible to the average person. The move has been toward more colloquial speech, not less. A second assumption follows: intelligibility of language is tied to relevance. As one compiler of contemporary worship resources advocated in 1968 in a collection entitled *Treat Me Cool, Lord*, to use archaic language in worship prevents prayer and worship from being relevant to real life and concerns.[6]

The linkage of intelligibility, accessibility, and relevance in contemporary worship has meant that its advocates have stretched the argument for contemporary language to encompass a range of liturgical features beyond words and Scripture. *Language* in the literature of contemporary worship has become a larger metaphor to argue for the necessity to contemporize other things so that the worship can speak to people today. Recent promoters of contemporary worship have spoken about the necessity of being contemporary with respect to the "languages" of music, graphic design, electronic multimedia (including movies), images (generally), or art.

SINGING SCRIPTURE

"Every true revival carries in its bosom a fresh love for and revelation upon the sacred Word." With this comment, the principal of a Pentecostal school in western New York (Elim Bible Institute) introduced the 1952 collection of new songs by a blind staff member of that school, Reta Kelligan.[7] The school had been caught up in a Pentecostal revival, the Latter Rain Movement, which had begun in some western provinces of Canada (Saskatchewan and British Columbia) in the late 1940s but soon spread across Canada

---

5. Lester Ruth, "How 'Pop' Are the New Worship Songs? Investigating the Levels of Popular Cultural Influence on Contemporary Worship Music," *Global Forum on Arts and Christian Faith* 3, no. 1 (2015), accessed July 11, 2016, http://www.artsandchristianfaith.org/index.php /journal/article/view/20/19.

6. Carl F. Burke, comp., *Treat Me Cool, Lord: Prayers—Devotions—Litanies as Prepared by Some of God's Bad-Tempered Angels with Busted Halos* (New York: Association Press, 1968), 14.

7. Reta Kelligan, *Scripture Set to Music* (Lima, NY: Elim Bible Institute, 1952), 3.

and the United States. Like Latter Rain outbreaks elsewhere, the revitalized Pentecostals in Lima, New York, felt led by God to new ways of worship, including pouring themselves into Kelligan's songs.

What was striking about her collection—and what made the principal refer to the Bible when introducing them—was that they were short biblical texts, mainly from the Psalms, set to music. Utilizing brief passages, Kelligan set them to simple musical forms and composed what would be called in later times "scripture choruses."

But Kelligan has not been the only contemporary songwriter to set scripture to music. Recently Matt Redman and Jonas Myrin used much of Psalm 103 as the core of their popular song, "10,000 Reasons." That they did so is not surprising. Redman, an internationally known composer, has been reported to say that the productivity of his songwriting is tied to how much time he spends reading scripture: the more immersed he is, the more the songs flow.[8]

In the sixty years between Kelligan and Redman other songwriters would agree. A use of scripture for song lyrics has been a critical way in which the Bible has been used in contemporary worship. This impact was especially strong in the early decades of the movement, reaching a pinnacle from the late 1960s to the mid-1980s. To sing scripture in simple choruses was a hallmark in the origins for contemporary worship.

No one represents this early impulse in contemporary worship better than David and Dale Garrett, a New Zealand couple who began compiling collections of scripture-set-to-music songs, known by the straightforward series title of *Scripture in Song*. Distribution in the United States began in the latter half of the 1970s: volume 1, *Songs of Praise* in 1975; volume 2, *Songs of the Kingdom* in 1981; and volume 3, *Songs of the Nations* in 1988. (See chapter 4 for more information.)

Examining the contents of these volumes confirms the truth-in-advertising of the series title. Each collection has about two hundred songs, the preponderance with lyrics drawn directly from short biblical passages of three verses or less. There is a strong King James Version influence on the lyrics as in the well-known chorus "Thou Art Worthy," drawn from Revelation 4:11. Old Testament passages predominate because of the large number of songs drawn from the Psalms. Other biblical books contributing larger numbers of songs include Revelation and Isaiah.

---

8. Lex Buckley, *Rise Up & Sing: Equipping the Female Worship Leader* (Colorado Springs: David C. Cook, 2010), 113–14.

But the Garretts were not the only source for singing scripture in contemporary worship's early years. For example, Chuck Smith, the pastor of Calvary Chapel in Costa Mesa, California, encouraged the young Jesus People songwriters in the congregation to write Bible-based choruses, which he used to teach this church how to sing scripture to music.[9] With his own capable voice, Smith himself sometimes led the singing.[10] This Bible emphasis shows up in an early published collection from this congregation, *Rejoice in Jesus Always* (1973), in which 20 percent of the songs are drawn from scripture. As in Kelligan's work and the *Scripture in Songs* volumes, the Psalms predominate. But other popular songs were drawn from elsewhere, like Karen Lafferty's "Seek Ye First," based on Matthew 6:33. This song was a mainstay for many years, including thirteen occurrences in the 1990s on top-25 song lists from Christian Copyright Licensing International (CCLI).

One congregation using "Seek Ye First" was John Wimber's Calvary Chapel of Yorba Linda/Anaheim (California) Vineyard congregation. (This church migrated between adjoining towns and also switched affiliations in its early years.) Records from this congregation indicate people actually sang scripture choruses. One service from 1982, for example, had four scripture songs out of sixteen total songs in the worship set. Similarly, this congregation's set of chord charts from the mid-1980s shows sixteen scripture songs out of this church's total repertoire of eighty-six songs.

To derive song lyrics from the scriptures has been a constant feature of contemporary worship over the years, as well-known songwriter Paul Baloche recently affirmed: "The most important thing if we're writing songs for worship is the Scriptures."[11] Whether in the earliest years or today, whether English- or Spanish-speaking, contemporary songwriters have used scriptures, especially Psalms, to find words for the church to sing.

What has changed is whether or not whole passages are set to music. Many early songs consisted only of short texts from the Bible. Over time, especially as the structures of the songs grew more complex, songs contained scriptural ideas and phrases without being limited to the biblical text. Some songs embody this evolution like Marty Nystrom's "As the Deer" (1986), which begins by closely reflecting Psalm 42 but expands beyond the biblical words. Paul Baloche's own "Your Name" (coauthored in 2006 with Glenn

9. Sharon Fischer, interview by Lester Ruth, March 7, 2015.

10. To hear Smith leading the congregation in "The Lord Bless Thee" from Numbers 6:24-26, accessed July 7, 2016, go to https://www.youtube.com/watch?v=R9LFXWVBYaI.

11. *Songwriting: The Journey of a Song*, with Paul Baloche (Lindale: Leadworship.com, 2011), DVD.

Packiam) goes a step further by fusing phrases from Psalm 65 and Proverbs 8. Hezekiah Walker is another example with songs like "The Lord Is my Shepherd" (based on Psalm 23) or "Let the Redeemed" (based on Psalm 107). Even though the use of scripture might be different, Reta Kelligan and her coworshippers at Elim Bible Institute would still recognize the desire to use God's word to worship God.

A BIBLICAL FOUNDATION FOR CONTEMPORARY WORSHIP

Scripture has also been used in the Pentecostal strand of contemporary worship to build a theological grounding for this approach to worship. Starting in the late 1940s, many Pentecostal adopters of contemporary worship constructed a biblical theology that provided a grounding for this emerging liturgical phenomenon. Initially the key Bible verses in this theology provided a sense of the reasonableness—even divine approval—of the features of this new way of worship. Over time as the theology became more multifaceted and more widespread, its teachers used it to teach contemporary worship as a divinely mandated pattern for worship. The eventual rise of musical worship sets with a determined form and purpose has been the most critical part of this pattern. (The category of "flow" as a critical part of this pattern was discussed in chapter 2; the interpretation of this teaching as a form of sacramentality will be considered in chapter 8.)

Whether in its early or later stages, this Pentecostal scriptural theology for contemporary worship achieved two ends. From a historical viewpoint, it expressed the latest impulse among some Protestants for what James White has called "liturgical Biblicism."[12] This biblicism has been a recurring feature in Protestantism whenever people have sought guidance in the scripture for shaping the form and actions of worship rather than in inherited, previous forms of worship (a liturgical "tradition"). The common questions from Protestants committed to this liturgical method have been "What is the biblical mandate for a form of worship?" and "What is the biblical example for a form of worship?" In the early Pentecostal development of contemporary worship, liturgical biblicism created a priority for praise as the central activity of an assembled congregation. This predilection for praise was musicalized and,

---

12.   See James F. White, *Protestant Worship: Traditions in Transition* (Louisville: Westminster John Knox Press, 1989).

combined with studies of the biblical words for *praise* and *worship*, became a pattern for how to order a service.

At the level of the actual worshippers, this Pentecostal biblical theology created a sense of stepping into an enactment of the biblical story. Its teachers did not construct it from abstractions but relied upon vivid biblical stories, especially from the Old Testament, to provide a visual representation of the sort of worship that God desired. The end was to portray contemporary worship as a fulfillment of God's desired trajectory for worship, culminating in the believers of Jesus Christ. This contemporary way of worship pleased God and facilitated an encounter with God. These notions, so prevalent in the Pentecostal literature on contemporary worship, are not developed or are missing in the materials of early mainline and evangelical proponents.

This Pentecostal literature shows an evolution over several decades as previous emphases provide the foundation for new levels of development. It is a story of how a renewed scriptural sense of the priority of praise developed into an established format for extended times of congregational singing as a "clear, biblical pattern" or "blueprint for a worship service."[13] Although the history of this story of Pentecostal biblical interpretation needs to be studied fully by scholars, it is still possible to sketch the broad parameters of its development. (See chapter 8 for more of this history.)

The first steps were a "discovery" of the importance of praise in the Bible and praise's connection to the presence of God. Reg Layzell, a Pentecostal preacher in western Canada swept up in the Latter Rain revival, was among the first—if not the first—to emphasize praise in this way. Taking Psalm 22:3 ("But thou art holy, O thou that inhabitest the praises of Israel" in the King James Version) as a divinely given launching point in 1946, Layzell began to preach exclusively on praise as his role grew in this revival of the late 1940s and 1950s.[14] His emphasis upon praise and his reliance upon Psalm 22:3 (along with other verses like Heb 13:15, Acts 16:23-25, Jonah 2:5-10, Ps 50:23, Ps 65:1, and Isa 60:18) would become standard features of Pentecostal teaching in the growth of a Pentecostal strand of contemporary worship.

The teaching evolved in the 1960s by the emergence of a kind of biblical typology in which structures for worship in the Old Testament—whether the tabernacle of Moses, the tabernacle of David, or the temple of Solomon— became a way of understanding the connection between praise and worship

---

13. Terry Law, *How to Enter the Presence of God* (Tulsa: Victory House Publications, 1994), 69.

14. Reg Layzell, *Unto Perfection: The Truth about the Present Restoration Revival* (Mountlake Terrace: The King's Temple, 1979), 120–21.

and the presence of God. Visualizing any of the structures enabled one to get a sense of step-by-step entering into the presence of God, encountering God ultimately in the holy of holies. Whether in this period or soon after, Psalm 100:4 became a common verse to gain a sense of this progression: "Enter into his gates with thanksgiving, and into his courts with praise: be thankful unto him, and bless his name" (KJV). David Fischer and Graham Truscott, teachers in this period, emphasized the Davidic tabernacle especially, allowing for a rich rationale for using the Psalms in Christian worship and highlighting David himself as an exemplary worshipper and worship leader. Terms like *Davidic worship and Psalmic worship* began to circulate.

The evolution of the Pentecostal rationale for contemporary worship picked up steam in the 1970s as the literature expanded. One prolific, popular author was Judson Cornwall, whose 1973 book, *Let Us Praise*, spoke about his own and his congregation's rediscovery of biblical praise and its importance. Like Layzell, he resolved to preach nothing but praise for a season.[15] In addition to Psalm 22:3 and Psalm 100:4, his book used visions of worship in Isaiah 6 and Revelation to describe the nature of true, biblical worship. All these passages became commonplace in the literature.

In the 1970s other Pentecostal authors pushed their biblical studies in ways that would also become common. Foremost among these developments were studies of the different Hebrew and Greek words for praise and worship in the Old Testament and New Testament respectively. Some studies nuanced the different shades of meanings in the various words to develop a multidimensional portrayal of biblical worship involving a range of expression, gestures, and postures. A critical, related development was distinguishing between praise and worship as distinct forms of reverencing God, an interpretive step taken by 1977 at least.[16] Building upon the architectural typology of tabernacles or temple, interpreted by the sequence of action words in verses like Psalm 100:4 (thanksgiving, praise), the groundwork was laid for transitioning *praise and worship* as a general term to a technical term outlining a biblical order for a service: first thanksgiving, then praise, and then worship.

By the early 1980s this step had been taken and, in an important move, was interpreted in a musical way. Thanksgiving, praise, and worship became a way of envisioning the ordering of songs in the time of congregational singing. The emerging biblical theology had been musicalized; Judson Cornwall's

---

15.   Judson Cornwall, *Let Us Praise* (North Brunswick: Bridge-Logos Publishers, 1973), 26.

16.   Thurlow Spurr, "Praise: More Than a 'Festival.' It's a Way of Life," *Charisma* 11, no. 6 (July/August 1977): 13.

writings demonstrate the evolution. In 1983, his book, *Let Us Worship*, acknowledged his growth in distinguishing between praise and worship and then used Psalm 100 and the tabernacle of Moses to speak about the worship set and worship leading.[17] His retrospective article from 1985 confirmed his sense of the novelty and growth of this type of contemporary worship in Pentecostalism since 1975 and especially since 1980.[18]

The latter half of the 1980s saw a growth in practical guides and conferences based on this musicalized biblical theology. The literature on this theology continued to be fine-tuned in the 1990s even as its constituent parts were in place. Some authors published pictorial representations, other writers tomes approaching systematic theological proportions, and others adoptions of the biblical theology for non-Pentecostal audiences.[19] Even though most of the available literature is from white authors, the range of ethnicities represented by its published proponents is evidence to the theology's spread, including African American and Hispanic churches.[20] The Pentecostal theological reflection has developed enough that overviews of it can now be offered.[21]

Regardless of decade or race, these Pentecostal authors share a method of biblical interpretation. Most of the biblical quotations are short with the exception of a few longer passages from the Old Testament offering important biblical typologies (e.g., 1 Chronicles 13–18). A stronger weight rests upon Old Testament passages than those from the New Testament. The interpreters tend to read across the Bible, connecting verses by typology and shared

---

17. Judson Cornwall, *Let Us Worship: The Believer's Response to God* (So. Plainfield: Bridge Publishing, 1983), 143, 153.

18. Judson Cornwall, "Trend toward Praise and Worship," *Charisma* 11, no. 1 (August 1985): 23–24.

19. Ruth Ann Ashton, *God's Presence through Music* (South Bend: Lesea Publishing Co., 1993); Ernest B. Gentile, *Worship God! Exploring the Dynamics of Psalmic Worship* (Portland: Bible Temple Publishing, 1994); and Don McMinn, *The Practice of Praise: A Handbook on Worship Renewal* (Irving, TX: Word Music, 1992).

20. African American: Myles Munroe, *The Purpose and Power of Praise & Worship* (Shippensburg, PA: Destiny Image Publishers, 2000); Rodney Williams Sr., *The Key of David: Davidic Patterns and Blueprints for Worship Leaders* (Plainfield, IL: Zion Musik, 2014), and Cheryl Wilson-Bridges, *Deeper Praise: Music, Majesty, or Mayhem* (Lake Mary, FL: Creation House, 2016); Hispanic: Marcos Witt, *Adoremos* (Miami: Editorial Caribe, 1993), and published in English as *A Worship-Filled Life* (Lake Mary, FL: Creation House, 1998), and Eddie Espinosa, "Worship" in *Let Your Glory Fall: Songs & Essays* (Worship & Revival Conference/Seminar Reader) (Anaheim, CA: Vineyard Music Group, 1995), 296–326.

21. Stephen R. Phifer, *Worship That Pleases God: The Passion and Reason of True Worship* (Victoria, BC: Trafford, 2005, 2014).

words, rather than settle into a single book. And there is a predilection for detailed studies of words like *praise* and *worship*, as noted above.

CONTEMPORARY PREACHING AND SERVICE PLANNING

If Pentecostal authors were developing a biblical theology for contemporary worship, mainline and evangelical authors focused on another task: examining what it meant to preach in a contemporary service. Indeed, the relative weight given to each of these biblical questions was a divide between most early Pentecostal and non-Pentecostal proponents of contemporary worship. The former focused on what made praise and worship biblically justifiable and facilitated an encounter with God; the latter concentrated on the manner of preaching the Bible that was most effective and enabled reaching new people.

Experimenting in preaching goes back to the earlier non-Pentecostal surge of contemporary worship in the late 1960s. The interest in homiletical experimentation was a part of early attempts at contemporary worship although it was not limited to contemporary services. A concern with whether previous forms of sermons still connected with people led to new forms across a range of churches and types of services. Even the World Council of Churches addressed the issue, encouraging sermons to be written with members of the congregation to increase their relevance to daily life and for sermons to include dialogue, drama, and visual arts.[22]

"Contemporary" preachers of the 1960s and 1970s tried a variety of new techniques. They preached dialogue sermons, either in active conversation with the congregation or with two preachers in dialogue with each other. Sermons included drama or were presented dramatically as first-person monologues from biblical characters. Some utilized technology to incorporate film or filmstrips into their sermons. Others included nonbiblical readings or based the sermon on pop music such as Don Williams's sermon on Bob Dylan's music preached at First Presbyterian Church in Hollywood.[23] How-to literature soon followed with titles like *Experimental Preaching* or *Creative Preaching.*[24]

---

22. Norman Goodall, ed., *The Uppsala Report 1968* (Geneva: World Council of Churches, 1968), 81–82.

23. Don Williams, *Call to the Streets* (Minneapolis: Augsburg Publishing House, 1972), 27.

24. John Killinger, ed., *Experimental Preaching* (Nashville: Abingdon Press, 1973); Elizabeth Achtemeier, *Creative Preaching: Finding the Words* (Nashville: Abingdon Press, 1980).

But the use of contemporary preaching in early contemporary services was not universal. In the important "new paradigm" churches[25] like Calvary Chapel, Hope Chapel, and Vineyard, their preachers (all with Pentecostal roots) followed more routine paths. Calvary Chapel's Chuck Smith preached expository sermons verse-by-verse through biblical books. Hope Chapel's Ralph Moore, influenced by Smith, followed his lead. And Vineyard's John Wimber excelled in biblical preaching on topics like the love of God.[26]

Regardless of the level of creative technique, successful contemporary sermons demonstrated two qualities that have characterized contemporary worship more broadly: a dedication to relevance regarding contemporary concerns in the lives of worshippers and a commitment to adapt in order to target intended listeners (see chapter 1). These qualities, seen in the literature about experimental preaching in the 1960s, surged in the 1990s through the writings of several preachers in prominent megachurches including Bill Hybels at Willow Creek Community Church (in Illinois), Walt Kallestad and Timothy Wright at Community Church of Joy (a Lutheran congregation in Arizona), and Rick Warren at Saddleback Church (in California). These preachers and their churches increased mainline and evangelical awareness of the alternative world of contemporary worship. They also provided the models and resources for one kind of appropriation of this worship: a tactical adoption to connect with new people.

At the time this approach to contemporary worship was characterized by a "seeker" label. People spoke of seeker-driven or seeker-sensitive variations among contemporary services.[27] Preachers expressed a seeker-orientation in several ways in their sermons or "messages" (if they wanted to avoid a word with potential negative connotations). One was a kind of "exegeting" of the targeted listeners to aim for relevance. A common way of undergirding this intentionality was to identify a felt need that the preacher would address. These contemporary preachers also developed sermons in short multiweek series,

25. The term *new paradigm* comes from sociologist Donald E. Miller in his book that studies these churches: *Reinventing American Protestantism: Christianity in the New Millennium* (Berkeley: University of California Press, 1997).

26. Chuck Smith, *Chuck Smith: A Memoir of Grace* (Costa Mesa: The Word for Today, 2009), 80–88; Ralph Moore, *Let Go of the Ring* (Honolulu: Straight Street Publishing, 1983), 51; Andy Park, Lester Ruth, and Cindy Rethmeier, *Worshiping with the Anaheim Vineyard: The Emergence of Contemporary Worship* (Grand Rapids: Wm. B. Eerdmans Publishing Co., 2017).

27. For an at-the-time review of these approaches, see Lester Ruth, "*Lex Agendi, Lex Orandi*: Toward an Understanding of Seeker Services as a New Kind of Liturgy," *Worship* 70, no. 5 (September, 1996): 386–405.

paying attention to normal cultural rhythms and providing eye-catching names for the series that spoke to immediate relevance or piqued curiosity. Felt needs often addressed in this approach were, not surprising, family, job, financial, and personal fulfillment issues. The cumulative effect created a sense that the narrative of an individual's personal life was the main arena for God's activity, not cosmic, systemic, or structural redemption. Dramatic skits reinforced the relevance of biblical themes to real life.

Even without a seeker label this sort of must-be-relevant preaching was widespread in non-Pentecostal contemporary services (and even in a few Pentecostal ones).[28] The overlap in homiletical approach arose from a tactical sense of targeting: services and sermons should be aimed at a particular sub-group of people. This evangelistically motivated approach to contemporary worship hit with a vengeance in the 1990s although it had antecedents, too, in youth-oriented experiments of the 1960s and earlier.[29]

One popular way to label targets was by generations, for example baby boomers or baby busters, as seen in one 1998 article: "This Is Not Your Father's Preaching Style: How To Speak the Language of the 'Whatever' Generation."[30] Church growth movement missiological theorists had begun advocating a generation-based approach to ministry by the late 1980s even though they had not picked up on the term *contemporary worship* yet. In the 1990s, however, generational targeting and advocacy for contemporary worship by that name became fused by these authors and others. Consultants, authors, and advocates gave attention to the perceived likes, interests, concerns, music, and worship capabilities of each age-defined group, suggesting that contemporary worship and preaching be targeted appropriately, depending upon the intended congregation. Most of this material assumed certain socioeconomic levels (seemingly middle class, suburban) and race (white). Comparable African American writings have been more explicit in acknowledging the racial dimension as well as tweaking the standard generational labels.[31]

---

28.   See Doug Murren, *The Baby Boomerang: Catching Baby Boomers as They Return to Church* (Ventura, CA: Regal Books, 1990), and Doug Murren, "Preaching to the Unchurched" in *Contemporary Worship: A Sourcebook for Spirited-Traditional, Praise and Seeker Services*, ed. Tim and Jan Wright (Nashville: Abingdon Press, 1997), 144–47.

29.   See Thomas E. Bergler, *The Juvenilization of American Christianity* (Grand Rapids: Wm. B. Eerdmans Publishing Co., 2012).

30.   Danny Harrell, "This Is Not Your Father's Preaching Style: How to Speak the Language of the 'Whatever' Generation," *Leadership* (Summer 1998): 83–86.

31.   F. Douglas Powe Jr., *New Wine New Wineskins: How African American Congregations Can Reach New Generations* (Nashville: Abingdon Press, 2012), 7–22.

Another general quality of contemporary worship that has increased in the last twenty years has been using electronic technology to help people visualize the word. As this commitment has developed, many churches, Pentecostal or non-Pentecostal, have incorporated visual elements into the act of preaching as well as developed visual graphics of the sermon's theme that are then utilized in multiple ways, usually by electronic projection.[32] Although incorporating visual elements was part of 1960s and 1970s preaching experiments (people at the time were concerned with the effect of watching TV on ability to hear sermons), the extent and sophistication of the most recent efforts exceed any earlier efforts. And this current visualizing of scriptural theme for a sermon or preaching series is more widespread across all contemporary worship. Having a technologically driven visualizing of the word seems more connected to the size of a church and its resources than to its denomination.

This resurgence in the use of visual media began in the mid-1990s just as mainline congregations were being hit with the promotion of contemporary worship by that name. Ginghamsburg United Methodist Church, for example, crossed its own threshold in 1994 as it moved into a new worship space with screens, projectors, and increased technological capabilities. Grasping the opportunity, the church's worship planners soon began experimenting to join the "Media Reformation."[33] Its staff would soon become advocates for this approach with a steady series of books and conferences by the late 1990s.[34] Gighamsburg's push was part of a wider wave of materials from the same time period as others pushed the necessity to increase the visual dimension in worship. Some, like Leonard Sweet, connected the push to portraying a new generation with having a postmodern perspective that was image- and story-driven.[35] By the early 2000s *multisensory* and *multimedia* had become buzzwords. Common visual elements related to scripture and its preaching have included thematic-related graphics, movie clips, in-house produced

---

32. An emerging scholar, Filip De Cavel, has suggested based on preliminary findings of his research that the desire to incorporate visuals shapes the sermon planning process and alters the content of the sermon, even at the last minute. Our thanks to him for noting this impact to us directly.

33. Michael Slaughter, *Out on the Edge: A Wake-Up Call for Church Leaders on the Edge of the Media Reformation* (Nashville: Abingdon Press, 1998), 76; Kim Miller, interview by Lester Ruth, February 5, 2016.

34. In addition to Michael Slaughter's writings (see immediately above), Kim Miller and Len Wilson have published multiple books.

35. Leonard Sweet, *Soul Tsunami: Sink or Swim in New Millennium Culture* (Grand Rapids: Zondervan, 1999), 17–18, 203, 209.

video, overlaid scripture verses, sermon bullet points, and projection of a camera shot of the preacher via IMAG (image magnification) so worshippers can still see her or his face clearly.

A team-based approach to worship planning has emerged for churches invested in visualizing the word. The starting point usually is the selection of a scripture and its main thematic point for the day. These initial choices are the prerogative of the preacher, who makes these decisions as stand-alone choices for a single service or, more typically, as part of a multiweek series on a topic. After these initial choices, however, a creative team takes up the responsibility for designing a service in which every dimension has been scripted to coordinate all the moving pieces needed to accomplish the actual worship service. At Impact Church in Atlanta, for example, pastor Olu Brown works with his Creative Programming team to design the Sunday "experience." This team itself is made up of four subteams: an administrative team (coordinating the behind-the-scenes technical and production items), a creative expressions team (dealing with the arts in worship), a service productive team (serving as directors or producers during the services), and a video production team (providing videography during a service and developing in-house video needed to support that day's message).[36] In this approach to contemporary worship, one can see contemporary worship's recurring traits: intelligibility, accessibility, creativity, and novelty.

Churches since the mid-2000s have been able to supplement their own in-house graphic and video production with materials obtained from companies and sharing websites. These companies and websites offer video illustrations, mini movies, worship song tracks, static and motion backgrounds for projection, and other graphics.

THE READ WORD IN CONTEMPORARY WORSHIP

In contrast to the increasing technological and planning complexity in many churches related to the scriptures, the Bible's actual use across a range of contemporary services remains simple. The main passage for the day will be read prior to the sermon. Other short passages might be read either by a musician if during the music set or by the preacher during the sermon. Worship planners and leaders make their own choices as to what scriptures to read.

---

36. Olu Brown et al., *Zero to 80: Innovative Ideas for Planting and Accelerating Church Growth* (Atlanta: Impact Press, 2010), 152.

That simplicity of practice and congregational freedom to choose means that a fully developed "service of the word" is almost never found in contemporary worship. In other words, to have multiple readings in close proximity and in a set sequence (Old Testament, Psalm, New Testament epistle, Gospel), found in a shared resource like a lectionary, is a rarity. Thus in the world of contemporary worship it is not the amount of Bible read in a service that makes worship scriptural, it is the other dimensions as described in this chapter.

Chapter 8
THE SACRAMENTALITY OF CONTEMPORARY WORSHIP

Throughout most of Christian worship history, notions of God's presence in worship have been closely associated with the Lord's Supper. Not surprisingly this meal has often been called either Communion (to reflect our fellowship with the Divine) or Eucharist (to name the gratitude that rightly accompanies such a gracious encounter). Sometimes in Christian history a sense of the word—the reading and preaching of scripture—has also occasionally picked up such sacramental notions. Centuries of Protestant congregations' experience indeed attest to God's presence in the word, as would the key Roman Catholic Vatican II document on worship, the Constitution on the Sacred Liturgy. In fact, until the development of specific, inclusive lists of sacraments in the twelfth century, a sense of God's presence and activity in multiple aspects of Christian worship was common. Thus, as the Constitution on the Sacred Liturgy notes, Jesus Christ is present in the church's worship, even when it prays and sings, based on his promise to be with two or three gathered in his name.[1]

Certain strands of contemporary worship have taken this connection between congregational singing and divine presence further than such a general affirmation. One of the distinctive elements of contemporary worship, especially in its Pentecostal expressions, has been to develop this idea of divine presence through congregational song into systems of theology and piety, which might be called *sacramental* if we allow this term to refer to a general notion of encounter with God's presence. This development within contemporary worship occurred with no dependence upon Catholic doctrine (of

---

1. Mary Ann Simcoe, ed., *The Liturgy Documents: A Parish Resource*, rev. ed. (Chicago: Liturgy Training Publications, 1985), 7 (chapter I.I.7 in the original document). Christ's promise occurs in Matthew 18:20.

course not!). It has relied, too, on a group of scriptures other than Christ's promise regarding two or three gathered.

A sign that a theological thought has developed and spread is when that idea can help frame job expectations for church staff. And so, perhaps a sure indication that associating God's presence with music has become widespread in contemporary worship is the expectation that the worship leader can facilitate the congregation's encounter with the divine by "ushering them into the presence of God." One worship scholar tells an anecdote to that effect. Relating the events at a pastor's conference in the late 1990s, the scholar noted that one pastor solicited applications for a musician's position by calling for someone who could "make God present through music."[2]

Making a special connection between music and divine presence has become so mainstream within contemporary worship that other writers have noted the same. And so they have written to describe this theological aspect of contemporary worship[3] or, occasionally, to provide it a stronger theological basis.[4] What is not available is a historical overview of the rise of this musical sacramentality. To fill that gap this chapter will describe the evolution of how this theology about the music of contemporary worship has developed. Where did it come from and how has it changed over time? How has God's presence come to be experienced as auditory? This chapter will answer those questions. We will also look at how other classic sacramental ideas associated with baptism and the Lord's Supper have sometimes showed up in contemporary worship. We will trace, too, the different levels of emphasis placed upon this musical sacramentality, suggesting that a lesser emphasis has been one of the ways in which mainline expressions of contemporary worship differs from Pentecostal or charismatic.

Noting the sacramentality of music within contemporary worship is important for several reasons. For one thing, knowing how the presence of God has become connected to congregational singing is an important window into Pentecostal versions of contemporary worship and how they differ from mainline manifestations. On a related note, this sacramental notion for worship music lies behind early methods of how to construct worship sets and

---

2. John D. Witvliet, "At Play in the House of the Lord: Why Worship Matters," *Books & Culture* 4, no. 6 (November/December 1998): 23.

3. Sarah Koenig, "This Is My Daily Bread: Toward a Sacramental Theology of Evangelical Praise and Worship," *Worship* 82, no. 2 (March 2008): 141–61.

4. Nick J. Drake, "Towards a Sacramental Understanding of Charismatic Sung Worship: The Mediation of God's Presence through Corporate Singing" (master's thesis, King's College London, 2008).

shape the order of worship. And understanding that sacramental notions have been attached to music helps us understand why baptism and the Lord's Supper have been relatively unimportant aspects of most forms of contemporary worship. If God was encountered in the music, they were not needed.

Finally, seeing the general absence of highly developed sacramental notions in mainline adoptions of contemporary worship establishes a vantage point from which to see some major differences between Pentecostal/charismatic contemporary worship and mainline manifestations of the same. Seeing these differences undercuts the simplistic historical explanations for—and complaints against—contemporary worship. Noting, too, the differences in mainline approaches to a liturgical phenomenon that in many ways has a Pentecostal genetic code can suggest ways in which mainline versions of contemporary worship have strengths and weaknesses.

PRAISE AND THE PRESENCE OF GOD

Take a survey asking people what biblical proof texts most strongly stand behind the rise of contemporary worship and there are bound to be a variety of answers. Many might point to "Sing to the Lord a new song" (Ps 96:1) since the movement has spawned the writing of so much new music. Others who have adopted contemporary worship to achieve greater effectiveness in evangelism might point to 1 Corinthians 9:22 ("I have become all things to all people") to support a willingness to try new styles in order to reach new peoples.

Both of those passages are possible contenders for the key biblical text behind the contemporary worship phenomenon. But there are two other possibilities that, in the writings of those involved in the early decades of the movement, are even more critical. Of these two passages the most vital would be Psalm 22:3, which states in the King James Version read by the early theorists for contemporary worship, "But thou art holy, O thou that inhabitest the praises of Israel." (Many recent translations speak of God being enthroned on the praises of Israel, a notion closely linked in some articulations of this theology.) Close behind the importance of Psalm 22:3 would be Psalm 100:4, which calls for worshippers to "enter God's gates with thanksgiving and God's court with praise." More than Psalm 96:1 or 1 Corinthians 9:22, it is these latter two passages, both individually and linked together, that form the biblical foundation upon which much of the early forms of contemporary worship were laid. In tandem the two provide the explanation for this new phenomenon. Psalm 22:3 gave the movement its rationale for emphasizing the praising of God and Psalm 100:4 offered a biblical grounding for a liturgi-cal order (from thanksgiving to praise to worship).

Together the two passages established a strong sense that God's presence could be experienced in a special way through corporate praising and that sequencing acts of worship in a certain way could facilitate the experiencing of divine presence and power. Once worshippers are aware of being in the presence of God, the natural response is one of adoring God. The roots for this line of teaching seemed to have first emerged in the late 1940s. By the 1980s the teaching had evolved into a system that could explain how and why sets of congregational songs should be put together in a certain way. In other words, by the 1980s the teaching had developed into a sacramental theology and piety explaining contemporary worshippers' liturgical experience of en-countering God in congregational singing during the worship set.

THE JOURNEY TOWARD A SACRAMENTALITY OF PRAISE

But that developed theological explanation was not where this line of pi-ety began. It started with a base notion of God's presence becoming manifest when Christians were praising. (Lest people scoff at this initial notion, the popular theologian, C. S. Lewis, once noted the same thing, although with no connection to Pentecostalism.)[5] It was at this beginning stage that Psalm 22:3 became a key biblical text within this emerging Pentecostal liturgical piety. This verse says, "But thou art holy, O thou that inhabitest the praises of Israel" (KJV)."

Perhaps the earliest evidence of this emphasis on Psalm 22:3 came in the Canadian-based Pentecostal revival known as the Latter Rain movement, as noted in chapter 7. One of the earliest participants, a minister by the name of Reg Layzell, whom some have called an "apostle of praise,"[6] wrote about a di-vine revelation in 1946 showing him the importance of this passage. The link between praising and God's presence was a particular part of the revelation, Layzell later wrote, testifying about a service in which he applied this promise

5. See C. S. Lewis, *Reflections on the Psalms* (New York: Harcourt, Brace and Company, 1958), 93.

6. Howard Rachinski, "From Praise to Worship" in *Restoring Praise & Worship to the Church*, ed. David Blomgren, Dean Smith, and Douglas Christoffel (Shippensburg, PA: Revival Press, 1989), 136.

of praise-induced presence.[7] According to Layzell, Psalm 22:3 was the key to experiencing God in the revival, and he became dedicated to the promotion of praise: "God burned that verse into me, and I preached nothing else but praise, praise, praise."[8]

Through the spread of the Latter Rain revival and its impact on mainline church's charismatic renewal movements, this teaching on praise spread widely and quickly. By the early 1970s, for example, the teaching, with its characteristic emphasis on Psalm 22:3, could be found in popular authors like the American Pentecostal teacher Judson Cornwall or the Chinese evangelical teacher Watchman Nee. Cornwall's statement that "the place of His [God's] dwelling is in the midst of the courtyard of praise" matched Nee's affirming that "though the throne of God is the heart of the universe, it is nonetheless established on the praise of the children of God."[9]

Common to these testimonies about the sacramentality of praise was a sense of a quality being restored to worship. This renewed sense of God's presence in worship was seen not only as a recovery of something from Pentecostal liturgical history but of something fundamentally biblical, too. These early, midcentury proponents of praise's sacramentality thus described scenes of praise and Presence reminiscent of their distant childhood. They also read back extended times of praise into the original Pentecost episode of Acts 2.

This initial emphasis on praise was about praise generally, not just musical praise. These early authors accentuated any sort of praise to God: sung, spoken, or shouted. God delighted in it all and responded to it by manifesting divine presence. Likewise, following biblical examples of people praising, physical expressions like raising hands and dancing were appropriate ways to honor God.[10] There was even a breadth in musical forms of praising. Various authors spoke highly of congregational song, instrumental music, or singing in the Spirit (i.e., unscripted singing of short phrases of praise or in tongues, having a chant-like quality and using spontaneous harmonization), this last element a hallmark of the Latter Rain revival and of many charismatic services at the time.

---

7.   Reg Layzell, *Unto Perfection: The Truth about the Present Restoration Revival* (Mountlake Terrace: The King's Temple, 1979), 11–13.

8.   Ibid., 120–21.

9.   Judson Cornwall, *Let Us Praise* (North Brunswick: Bridge-Logos Publishers, 1973), 25; Watchman Nee, *Assembling Together* (New York: Christian Fellowship Publishers, Inc., 1973), 109.

10.   Graham Truscott, *The Power of His Presence: The Restoration of the Tabernacle of David* (Burbank: World Map Press, 1969), 236–58.

And praise was fitting to congregations assembled for worship as well as individuals. In congregations praising God could be a joint effort, as in a song, or it could come from a time of all worshippers vocalizing what was on their heart, speaking all at once. Other literature like the popular books of Merlin Carothers, a military chaplain, spoke of praise as the centerpiece of an individual's daily lifestyle, complete with the sense of God's presence. Even in this literature on individual praise and God's presence Psalm 22:3 remained the key link between the two.[11]

Over the next decades this base notion about praise's sacramentality developed, expanded, and changed. One early step, almost simultaneous with the initial linking of praise and God's presence, was to fuse a sense of this presence with God's power. Where God is, God acts. Where God acts, God does so in power. This linkage of divine presence and power expressed a basic sensibility in Pentecostal piety highlighting God as One eager to act dramatically in the world today. That fusion sometimes led to strong instrumental and causal notions for praise: to have God show up and act, Christians should praise. Thus Layzell's 1952 proclamation that through praise "we produce or release the presence of the captain of the Lord's army" was affirmed through a simpler formula from 1975: "praise is power."[12] Other common ways to express the same sentiment was to speak of praise as a weapon of spiritual warfare or to note that the coming of God through praise opened up worship as a time for God to exhibit "signs and wonders."

Another early development, overlapping and intertwining with the first two, was linking this root notion of the sacramentality of praise with architectural categories drawn from considering the Old Testament tabernacles (either Moses's or David's) or temple (Solomon's). This architectural connection was being taught by the late 1960s, at least, and soon found its ways into published form. Guided by verses like Psalm 100:4, authors interpreted the various areas of these structures to provide a template for placing praise within a larger liturgical framework. Specifically, praise became associated with thanksgiving and worship, within a larger concern of God's presence connected to the inner sanctums of either the tabernacle or temple.

Thus this architectural overlay developed the teaching about praise's sacramentality in two ways. First, because God's presence was associated with the inner sanctums of the various Old Testament structures, this typology placed

---

11. Merlin R. Carothers, *Power in Praise* (Escondido: Merlin R. Carothers, 1972), 12.

12. Reg Layzell, *The Pastor's Pen: Early Revival Writings of Pastor Reg. Layzell*, comp. B. Maureen Gaglardi (Vancouver: Glad Tidings Temple, 1965), 94; Paul E. Billheimer, *Destined for the Throne* (Fort Washington, PA: Christian Literature Crusade, 1975), 120.

praise as part of a journey of worshippers moving toward God's presence. Just as a historical figure would have started outside the tabernacle of Moses, for example, using a basic sense of going from outside to the inner holy of holies, a Christian congregation would move toward God's presence as it transitioned from acts of thanksgiving to praise to worship. Different forms of that basic teaching began to be published by at least the early 1970s, as in Judson Cornwall's popular 1973 book, *Let Us Praise*.[13]

The approach was a common one in the late twentieth century, remaining to the present day, although its appeal had begun to wane among some as early as the 1980s. One popular variation of the teaching was to emphasize the tabernacle of David, not of Moses. This focus was popular with some praise advocates because the perceived lack of animal sacrifice in David's tabernacle—as compared to the Mosaic tabernacle or the temple of Solomon—enabled these Pentecostal teachers to make an easier connection to Christian worship by emphasizing a sacrifice of praise instead. In this way David's example could even be labeled as "New Testament" with David lifted up as exemplary type for Christian worshippers.[14] This emphasis on David made looking at praise and worship in the Psalms especially appropriate.

The increased focus on the Psalms became part of the next development in the teaching about praise's sacramentality. The step of linking praise to Old Testament liturgical architecture became part of a surge in Pentecostal literature on word studies of biblical words for praise, worship, and related concepts. These word studies systematized the scriptural terms, emphasizing the nuances of different meanings and organizing them into a biblical rationale for this renewed way of Pentecostal worship, especially its emphases on praise, expressiveness, intensity, and physical movement. Praise advocates quickly developed a standard list of words, a list still found in some recent expressions of this teaching, such as Rodney Williams Sr.'s recent book.[15] Because so many words in this list had some connotation of bodily posture or movement in the original Hebrew or Greek, the emphasis on bodily expression and movement—even dance—seemed biblically justifiable.

This deeper reflection on the biblical words evolved into a critical development in the literature: making a distinction between the words *praise* and

---

13. Cornwall, *Let Us Praise*, 24.

14. One example is David E. Fischer, "King David's 'New Testament' Worship" in *Restoring Praise & Worship to the Church,* ed. David Blomgren, Dean Smith, and Douglas Christoffel (Shippensburg, PA: Revival Press, 1989), 9-17.

15. Rodney Williams Sr., *The Key of David: Davidic Patterns and Blueprints for Worship Leaders* (Zion Musik, 2014), 12.

worship. Two important books by Judson Cornwall provide a time bracket for this development. Although his 1973 book, *Let Us Praise*, did not distinguish between the two words, his 1983 book, *Let Us Worship*, did. Cornwall noted that he had learned to tell the two apart in the intervening years, now seeing that "praise is the vehicle of expression that brings us into God's presence, but worship is what we do once we gain an entrance to that presence."[16] From the early 1970s to the early 1980s, other authors increasingly drew a distinction between the two words as ways of vocally honoring God. Not only were the two words distinguished as liturgical words, authors advocated a certain proper sequence to them: praise precedes worship as Cornwall himself noted: "We traverse God's courts with praise, but when we are drawn into the holy place with God, worship is the prescribed response."[17] Psalm 100:4 and other passages related to Old Testament architecture for worship provided the rationale for telling between the two words.

An important result was that the phrase *praise and worship* no longer had a general meaning of corporately honoring God—as it had had previously—but itself became a technical phrase designating this new approach to Pentecostal liturgy. The earliest books teaching the sacramentality of praise had used the term in a general way. And so it was possible for these earlier authors to even invert the term and occasionally speak of *worship and praise*. But with the growing distinction made between the two terms by the late 1970s, that inversion was no longer possible. The phrase became a technical one with each term having its own nuance of meaning, as musician Thurlow Spurr noted in a popular Pentecostal magazine:

> Praise and worship are not the same. Praise is thanking God for the blessings, the benefits, the good things. It is an expression of love, gratitude, and appreciation. Worship involves a more intense level of personal communication with God, centering on His person. In concentrated worship, there is a sort of detachment from everything external as one enters God's presence.[18]

And there was an assumed order to the two as the teaching developed: first praise and then worship.

---

16. Judson Cornwall, *Let Us Worship: The Believer's Response to God* (So. Plainfield: Bridge Publishing, 1983), 149.

17. Ibid., 61.

18. Thurlow Spurr, "Praise: More Than a 'Festival.' It's a Way of Life," *Charisma* 11, no. 6 (July–August 1977): 13.

Simultaneously, on a parallel track, close consideration of praise and worship attracted Pentecostal teachers to the passages in the biblical book of Revelation that show scenes of worship before the throne of God. Where might this praise and worship be seen? In heaven, of course. Associating the church's praise and worship with that of heaven reinforced thoughts of human participation in angelic worship with its intensity, perpetuity, and focus on God's holiness, all themes reflected in the literature and in the growing body of "praise and worship" songs. The association also reinforced the cosmic dimensions of praise with it being considered as part of spiritual warfare against the realm of evil.

All of these initial steps were in place by the early 1980s. What that decade brought was an increasing musicalization to all of these notions. Although there had always been a liturgical dimension to the teaching of praise's sacramentality, the 1980s became a time when the focus of this theology narrowed to thinking of it primarily as theology and piety about corporate worship. Simply put, "praise and worship," with all of its developed notions of the means of encountering God's presence, became a way of worship that could be taught and promoted. Not surprisingly, literature of the 1980s began to speak in detail about how to construct a set of worship songs: begin with songs of thanksgiving, transition to songs of praise, and, once in God's presence, sing worship songs. Indeed some of the songs from the period seem expressly written to provide a map along this affection- and music-based entrance rite. Songs like "I will enter His gates with thanksgiving in my heart / I will enter his courts with praise" (from 1976) or "We bring the sacrifice of praise into the house of the Lord" (from 1984) seem written to facilitate the musical journey through Old Testament liturgical architecture.

Again Judson Cornwall's writing provides some background to see timing of the historical development. Although his 1983 book has a section on how to construct a set of songs fitting a praise and worship, tabernacle-based paradigm, he continued to use some older terminology, for example, *song leader* and *song service*, that showed older Pentecostal sensibilities.[19] The growing body of literature on how to do musical praise and worship would shift increasingly to the newer terminology (like *worship leader* and *worship set*) along with being concerned with organizing songs so as to achieve a flow of praise and worship. Indeed, by the late 1980s, Pentecostal teacher Barry Griffing, who had been instrumental with his brother Steve in leading an important teaching venue on worship in the 1970s and 1980s called the International

---

19. Cornwall, *Let Us Worship*, 153–58.

Worship Symposium, was arguing ardently that Pentecostals ought to set aside their preference for spontaneity and instead plan an order for congregational singing. Planning was to take into consideration the key and tempo of songs as well as where a song lyrically fit in the journey to experience the "presence of Christ as He manifests Himself through prophecy and power."[20] Considering key, tempo, and lyrical fit of songs with respect to thanksgiving, praise, and worship became a dominant task of the church musician, now dubbed the worship leader. The literature on how to construct such sequences of songs mushroomed as evidenced by books like Pentecostal author Ruth Ann Ashton's 1993 work, *God's Presence through Music*. The sequencing of thanksgiving, praise, and worship continued to be a way of conceiving of a Christian lifestyle, too, as seen in the writings of Marcos Witt, an important Hispanic Pentecostal worship leader and songwriter.[21]

Even when the precise temple/tabernacle typologies or praise-to-worship model were not used, these early practitioners of contemporary worship developed alternative approaches for constructing an order of worship songs, that is, a worship set. For example, in the mid-1980s at the Anaheim Vineyard congregation, the mother church of the Vineyard Fellowships, pastor John Wimber worked with the worship leader Eddie Espinosa to morph Vineyard's earlier sense of distinguishing between singing about God (roughly analogous to songs of thanksgiving and praise) to singing to God (analogous to songs of worship) into a five-phase pattern: invitation, engagement, intimacy, visitation (of God), and giving of substance (i.e., the worshipper's self-giving to others). (Note that Espinosa had grown up in a church in which Psalm 22:3 and the tabernacle of David had been important parts of the instruction on worship.[22]

Regardless of which model was used, the role and title of a congregation's chief musician had taken on special significance as the 1980s unfolded. No longer were these musicians simply known as music ministers or song leaders; they were now *worship leaders*, a term that began to circulate among

20. Barry Griffing, "Releasing Charismatic Worship" in *Restoring Praise & Worship to the Church*, ed. David Blomgren, Dean Smith, and Douglas Christoffel (Shippensburg, PA: Revival Press, 1989), 94–98.

21. Ruth Ann Ashton, *God's Presence through Music* (South Bend, IN: Lesea Publishing Co., 1993); Marcos Witt, *A Worship-Filled Life* (Orlando: Creation House, 1998), originally published in Spanish as *Adoremos* (Miami: Editorial Caribe, 1993).

22. John Wimber, "Worship: Intimacy with God" in *Thoughts on Worship* (Anaheim, CA: Vineyard Music Group, 1996), 4–6; Eddie Espinosa, interview by Lim Swee Hong and Lester Ruth, May 2, 2015.

Pentecostals around 1980. The term caught on quickly enough so that by 1985 Judson Cornwall was noting the recent popularity of "upgrading" the title of song leader to this new term.[23] The role of the worship leader was explicitly critical by the late 1980s: this was the person who would "bring the congregational worshippers into a corporate awareness of God's manifest Presence."[24] Or, as the pastor at the beginning of the chapter put it colloquially, a worship leader's job was to "make God present through music." The sacrament of musical praise had been established.

What has happened since the early 1990s? Within Pentecostalism, especially among white Pentecostals, there seems to have been a dissipating of this teaching about the sacramentality of praise although vestiges still remain. What have not waned are the root sentiments behind this theology of sacramental praise: a desire to encounter the divine through music and a sense that when God is present God is present in active power. And among Asian, Latino, and African American Pentecostals, the earlier, more precise teaching about the sacramentality of praise seems to be lingering longer. The dividing line seems to be continued use of the term *praise and worship*. Those churches which still use this term—Pentecostal or not—seem to be the places where the older teaching remains.

On the other hand, white mainline congregations who adopted contemporary worship in the 1990s largely did so on a different model and under a different name. While there were some inroads among white mainlines in the early part of that decade of "praise and worship"—the June 1991 theme issue of *Reformed Worship* and some reflections by worship speaker Robert Webber were probably the highway mark—by and large white mainline and evangelical Christians adopted contemporary worship for tactical reasons. Whereas the Pentecostal approach had been to adopt the new music as a way of encountering God, these congregations tended to implement contemporary worship as a strategic way of attracting new people. Both the writings of and our interviews with early white adopters show this evangelical motivation. What the white adopters do not show is as clear and precise sense of praise's sacramentality as did the early Pentecostal teachers There might be a general sense of encountering God through the music of contemporary worship among white mainline worshippers but not the specificity of the developed Pentecostal theology for the same.

---

23. Bob Sorge, e-mail message to Lester Ruth, January 30, 2016. Judson Cornwall, *Elements of Worship* (South Plainfield: Bridge Publishing, Inc., 1985), 131.

24. Griffing, "Releasing Charismatic Worship," 92.

OTHER SACRAMENTAL DIMENSIONS

If the presence of God has been one of the central sacramental notions for the Eucharist in the history of the church, another has been a sense that this sacrament is also a sacrifice, although opinions differ widely among past and present Christians about how the sacrament is sacrificial. Similarly, Pentecostal theorists of contemporary worship have emphasized the praising of God as sacrificial although they have emphasized different meanings for this idea. At least four can be found in Pentecostal and charismatic writings about praise and worship. All four can be found in discussions of both corporate praising as well as in description of the inward posture and activity of individual Christian disciples. This breadth is evidence of how critical praise became in late twentieth century Pentecostalism.

One approach has been to make the phrase *sacrifice of praise* synonymous with a congregation praising God. Thus some of the descriptions about the Latter Rain revival, which stands behind so much of the increased emphasis on praise among Pentecostals and charismatics in the late twentieth century, simply speak of congregations engaged in a sacrifice of praise when describing the focused, intense, and extensive periods of corporate praising, spoken and sung.

Another interpretation of praise as sacrifice has been to emphasize praise as an act of obedience to God's explicit command in the Bible. Reg Layzell spoke of this dimension as have others.[25] A verse commonly mentioned is Hebrews 13:15, which commands continually offering a sacrifice of praise to God. By emphasizing praise as an act of obedience to an explicit biblical command, this interpretation highlights the propriety of praise as an act of the will beyond an individual's feelings or desire.

From this emphasis on the propriety of praising regardless of feelings comes the third line of teaching about the sacrifice of praise. This third interpretation emphasizes the costly nature of sacrifice in speaking about the propriety or necessity of praising God even in times of distress, grief, or great trouble.[26] The distress might be relatively minor, as in the case of feeling foolish by expressing praise in front of other worshippers, or major as when praising God in the midst of a loved one dying.

---

25. Layzell, *The Pastor's Pen*, 104; Graham Truscott, *The Power of His Presence: The Restoration of the Tabernacle of David* (Burbank, CA: World Map Press, 1969), 277–84.

26. For examples, see the writings of Terry Law: *The Power of Praise and Worship* (Tulsa, OK: Victory House, Inc., 1985), 166, or *How to Enter the Presence of God* (Tulsa, OK: Victory House, Inc., 1994), 79.

A final line of interpretation has been to emphasize the difference between sacrifices of animals and the sacrifice of praise. This teaching emerges in those authors who use the tabernacle of David, rather than the tabernacle of Moses or the temple of Solomon, as the structure that provides the typological grid for interpreting the approach to God through praise and worship. Since no animal sacrifices were offered in David's tabernacle—so the teaching goes—it is the sacrifice of praise, seen in multifaceted ways through all of David's psalms, that provide the type for Christian contemporary worship.[27]

Hebrews 13:15 (let us continually offer a sacrifice of praise) provides another link to broadly Eucharistic echoes: the idea that the sacrifice is to be *offered* to God. While this notion of offering something to God in the Lord's Supper might be foreign or objectionable to much Protestant piety, the idea itself is a longstanding one in the history of worship. It reaches all the way back to the earliest centuries of the church, being found in various modes of expression across the centuries as offering praise and thanksgiving, the Eucharistic food, or ourselves. What is common is the root thought that the sacrament is a time for ministering to God, not simply receiving something from God. Consequently, the furniture around which this activity takes places is rightly called an *altar* and not just a *table*. By the late Middle Ages theology about the Eucharist as sacrifice offered to God had developed to a sophisticated degree although at the level of popular piety such nuances were lost. Thus the sacrificial aspects of the Eucharist as offered to God were seen as effectively instrumental: it was a propitiation that brought about desired results from God to the people.

Early Protestant Reformers routinely rejected such medieval sacrificial notions. Either they emphasized the sacrament as a gift from God to us (that sounds a lot less like works righteousness) or they thought of it as strictly human activity to remind us of God's saving activity at another time and place. Removed from the immediate turmoil of the Protestant Reformation, later centuries have allowed Protestants to recover something of a more dynamic sense of Eucharistic sacrifice. And so the recent revisions of the United Methodist Great Thanksgiving, for example, have the congregation agreeing to offer themselves "in praise and thanksgiving as a holy and living sacrifice in union with Christ's offering for us."

In the sacramentality of praise and worship, these Eucharistic notions of worshippers offering themselves in praise as a living sacrifice become attached

---

27. David E. Fischer, "King David's 'New Testament' Worship" in *Restoring Praise & Worship to the Church*, ed. David Blomgren, Dean Smith, and Douglas Christoffel (Shippensburg, PA: Revival Press, 1989), 9–17.

to the raw act of praise, not the Lord's Supper. It is an attachment that emerged early and repeatedly in the literature. Indeed, many writers speak of the mid-twentieth century as a time when God was restoring this dimension to the church's worship. The praise that God's people lift up, especially in singing, is an offering to the Lord. The authors often frame this notion of offering praise as a priestly activity of Christians, drawing upon not only New Testament Scriptures that speak of Christians having a priestly identity but also of the typologies drawn from the tabernacles or Temple of the Old Testament. As the people enter into God's presence by praising, they arrive at a symbolic point at which they minister to God or, as some say it, to offer praise to the "heart of God." Except for the heart language, much of this explanation could be applied to many historical understandings of the sacrament of the Eucharist.

As the idea of the sacramentality of praise developed, it usually picked up another quality that has characterized understanding of the Eucharist: a confidence in its instrumental effectiveness. In other words, the sacrament achieves what it symbolizes. While developed praise and worship thinkers would not consider praise to be symbolic, still a similar sort of instrumental confidence would apply to how they saw praise operating. When God's people praise, God will be present. The teachers of praise and worship are confident in this instrumental effectiveness for praise. By the time of the high-water mark of this teaching in the 1980s and early 1990s, the confidence was evident in book titles (e.g., *God's Presence through Music*), statements (e.g., "praise and worship is one of the simplest forms of entrance into the presence of God"), and church musician job searches (we want someone who can "make God present through music," to reference the earlier anecdote).[28]

A similar sort of confidence with respect to sacraments generally—and to the Eucharist specifically—had developed in the history of the Western church, reaching its own kind of high-water mark in the scholastic theology of the late Middle Ages. From the late patristic period for the next thousand years, sacramental theologians had perfected a theology that confidently spoke of the sacraments as the occasions for God's presence and activity. By the scholastic medieval period, theologians spoke in definitive terms of God as the primary actor in the administration of a sacrament, not people, thus making the inward disposition of human worshippers less important. Resting upon God's character, this approach to the sacraments could be sure of the Eucharist's instrumental effectiveness.

---

28. Respectively, see Ashton, *God's Presence through Music*, Kent Henry, "Worship's Current Phases and Future Trends," *The Psalmist* (April–May 1988): 6, and Witvliet, "At Play in the House of the Lord," 23.

What lay behind the Pentecostal confidence in praise's instrumental effectiveness was not as much a highly developed theology as it was a critical aspect of Pentecostal (and evangelical) piety: the belief that God will always be true to explicit divine promises found in the Bible. Interpret Psalm 22:3 not as a poetic statement but as a divine promise to be trusted and one has gone a long way toward an instrumental efficacy for praise. Add the Pentecostal notions that where God is, God acts, and that God acts in power, and one has arrived at that affirmation. This theology had spread widely by the 1970s, a thought affirmed in prose ("It is, of course, a fact that when we honestly praise God, something *does* happen as a result") and song ("Praise the Lord / For our God inhabits praise").[29]

Because of Pentecostalism's emphasis on affections and emotions in worship, its approach to the instrumental aspect of praise's sacramentality would never have the same objectivity as medieval theologies about the Eucharist. But it could have some objective quality. And so the theorists behind the sacramentality of praise could make a case that real praise, too, that is obedient to the Bible (and thus an effective instrument) is a matter of each worshippers' will, not his or her emotions, as Reg Layzell stated in 1952:

> Real Scriptural praise and worship is something that has faith in it; something in which the will is brought into action. Real praise is more than a sentimental human feeling. . . . Those who offer praise in spirit do so with the full intent of the will and full assurance of faith which is expressed in complete obedience to the Word of God, feelings or no feelings.[30]

Indeed, so confident was the theology that praising brought about the active presence of God in worship that later writers took time to explain the difference been God's constant presence everywhere and the presence experienced during times of worship. A common approach was to make a difference between divine omnipresence and the manifest presence experienced in praise and worship.

With such a strong sense of praise's instrumentality in bringing about God's active presence, a teaching spreading widely from a variety of sources, other authors begin to warn Pentecostal worshippers about praising only to receive something good from God. These cautionary voices continued to affirm praise's effectiveness with God but advised contemporary worshippers to always be more interested in the Giver than in the gift. Worshippers should

---

29. Carothers, *Power in Praise*, 6; The Imperials, "Praise the Lord" on their *Heed the Call* album, 1979.

30. Layzell, *The Pastor's Pen*, 104.

not praise "with an eye secretly looking for the expected results"[31] but should make sure their praise leads to worship because worship is more than asking. It is admiring.[32]

A sign that the acceptance of praise's instrumental effectiveness with God had been accepted widely was the acceptance of this teaching into the sub-branch of Pentecostal thinking known as the prosperity gospel. Articulated by a prosperity proponent, praise's effectiveness was not simply a trusting acceptance of God's presence and activity but a tool of faith to be wielded for the worshipper's benefit. As one author exulted in 1976, "Praise is for us.... 'Prayer asks but praise takes. Prayer talks about the problem but praise takes the answer from God.'"[33] To be fair, most of the proponents of praise's sacramentality do not express their theology in such aggressive, self-serving ways but keep the focus on God, who is rightly worshipped and appreciated.

Two final aspects of Eucharistic associations can be found in the theology of the sacramentality of musical praise. One is the commemorative, or anamnetic, quality of thanksgiving and praise. In the Lord's Supper this aspect was central to the prayer of consecration itself. In all the prayer's classic forms, even those versions reaching back to the early church, a central feature was thanksgiving and praise to God achieved by reciting God's mighty acts of creation and salvation.

In contemporary worship a similar sacramental emphasis on commemoration has been achieved whenever there has been close parsing of biblical words for *thanksgiving* or *praise* as compared to *worship*. This parsing was especially evident in the word studies of different biblical words for worshipping God. Sometime around the 1970s praise and worship apologists quit using *praise and worship* as a general term for a congregational service, as it had been understood, and began instead to distinguish praise from worship as discussed in chapter 7.

Once this distinction began to be made, commentators usually placed a strong commemorative aspect on praise. Praise was about remembering God's nature and activity, past and present, honoring him on that basis. (Thanksgiving could have those associations, too.) Praise established the contact with

31. Carothers, *Power in Praise*, 6.

32. Cornwall, *Let Us Worship*, 145–46.

33. Charles Trombley, *How to Praise the Lord* (Harrison: Fountain Press, 1976), 49, 77. On p. 77 Trombley is paraphrasing a quote from E. W. Kenyon. For a placement of praise within a larger assessment of prosperity thinking, see Kate Bowler and Wen Reagan, "Bigger, Better, Louder: The Prosperity Gospel's Impact on Contemporary Christian Worship," *Religion and American Culture: A Journal of Intepretation*, 24, no. 2 (Summer 2014): 186–230.

God's presence. Worship, on the other hand, was what happened as people responded to being in the divine presence. Worship thus centered on direct adoration of the person of God. As one Pentecostal author put it recently, "Praise is the expression of thanksgiving to the Lord and the exaltation of the Lord that brings us into His presence, [while] worship is the expression of submission to God, adoration of Him, and commitment to Him."[34]

Similar to its anamnetic quality, praise understood sacramentally has also had an epicletic dimension in praise and worship. The epiclesis in Eucharistic prayers is the petitioning of God to send the Holy Spirit in the sacrament. There is a strong, recurring similarity in contemporary worship's music although the desired divine coming is not as tightly focused on the Holy Spirit's coming. Throughout contemporary worship's history there has been a strong desire (and expectation) that God would come, both in terms of Christ's return and, especially, of God's arrival in corporate worship. The name of one of the original music companies (Maranatha! Music, which means "Come, Lord" in first-century Aramaic) verbalized this dimension.

But the real evidence of the epicletic, sacramental quality of contemporary worship is how common the petitioning in song for God (or Jesus or the Spirit) to come in worship. *Come* is one of the most used verbs in the lyrics of contemporary worship songs. Among the most popular songs, it stands equal with *save* as the most common divine actions.[35]

A related way, especially in Pentecostal circles, for expressing this epicletic quality of contemporary worship, including the music, is to speak of an anointing on or in worship. Although a widespread term, it is also a vague one having a variety of different meaning. Its basic thrust is to affirm a perceived sense of the Holy Spirit, whether it is the community's or an individual's discernment of the Spirit's special touch. To affirm that contemporary worship has been anointed is to feel as if the Spirit has come upon it. The theorists for its sacramentality confess that this anointing is often the case. As one stated it, praise and worship "combine the anointing of three different vehicles for contact with God: God's Word, God's Spirit, and God's music."[36] This anointing is indeed an epiclesis fulfilled.

Most of the dimensions of musical sacramentality have struck tones that are Eucharistic. But there is one aspect of music's sacramentality that is as

---

34. Stephen R. Phifer, *Worship That Pleases God: The Passion and Reason of True Worship* (Victoria, BC: Trafford Publishing, 2005, 2014), 36–37.

35. Lester Ruth, "Some Similarities and Differences between Historic Evangelical Hymns and Contemporary Worship Songs," *The Artistic Theologian* 3 (2015): 83.

36. Henry, "Worship's Current Phases and Future Trends," 6.

reminiscent of baptismal themes as it is of Eucharistic ones: the role of music in creating a sense of unity. As others have noted, music has played an important social function in the history of contemporary worship. Attachment to a style of music has become a way of identifying one's self and stating to which group one belongs.[37] It is thus also a way of stating to whom one does not belong. It is group unity based on musical style. The style gathers, joins together, and excludes those who have not accepted the style. In this way choosing a contemporary worship service, whatever its particular form of popular music, was roughly equivalent to the renunciations and professions of allegiance that take place in a baptismal service. As baptismal candidates are called upon to renounce certain allegiances and adhere to Christ and his church, worshippers choosing popular styles of music often were making statements about who they identified with in terms of church, what the shared values of the group were with respect to the worship of God, and what they were rejecting in terms of worship and other people.

Music's social function in group unity is also seen in the refusal to stream the music in multisite church campuses. Recent technological advances in streaming have allowed larger contemporary worship churches to link their multiple campuses in worship. Typically, however, it is not the music but the sermon that is provided from a central location. The dynamics of live, embodied music—but not preaching—seem important for creating the sense of a congregation having actually assembled to worship.

Music's role in a kind of sacramental unifying was also seen in how debates over musical style fueled the fighting during the worship wars. As tensions flared in the 1990s when mainline congregations in increasing numbers began to adopt contemporary worship, a main field of conflict became arguments about what style of music was appropriate for Christian worship. Music's social, sacramental function in creating group unity became evident as factions gathered by musical style to fight each other.

VARYING LEVELS OF SACRAMENTAL DISCERNMENT

Recognizing contemporary worship music's sacramentality, especially a sense of connecting praise to God's presence, is not an even phenomenon

---

37. Michael S. Hamilton, "A Generation Changes North American Hymnody," *The Hymn* 52, no. 3 (July 2001): 16. Recent ethnographic looks at contemporary worship music also highlight how the music can create a sense of community beyond a single worshipper's congregation.

across the breadth of churches practicing contemporary worship. This sort of sacramental piety, expressed in specific terms with detailed theological reflection, is much more a Pentecostal view on contemporary worship than a mainline Protestant one. Almost all white, mainline materials from the 1990s disregard the theology of praise and worship—its "robust pneumatology," to use the words of Matthew Sigler—while the songs and the style themselves became the focus.[38] The different phrases *praise and worship* and *contemporary worship*, the former more prevalent in Pentecostal circles and the latter in white mainline circles, mark a boundary line for the level of recognizing worship music's sacramentality. It was as if white mainline congregations adopted the interface for contemporary worship (its style) for tactical reasons without also appropriating its operating system (its emphasis upon the Spirit and the sacramentality of praise). Consequently, Pentecostals have developed a richer body of teaching and literature on the spirituality of contemporary worship whereas mainline authors have written more on the evangelistic uses of contemporary worship as well as on specific topics like preaching and the use of media.

The Pentecostal/white mainline difference also showed itself in the model for adoption of contemporary worship. Because they often started contemporary worship services for tactical reasons to reach new people, white mainliners frequently added a contemporary service to their weekend schedule, creating a range of services based on style. That was the context in which the term *contemporary worship* originated and became sensible. Pentecostals, on the other hand, have been more likely to transform their whole way of worship—rather than add stylistically different services—as they have fine-tuned their ways of worship to better fulfill the theological rationale of sacramentality.

Another difference is how the history of contemporary worship has been told. Whereas Pentecostal authors have spoken of its rise in terms of divine gift, revelation, or revival, mainline historians usually have told the story of the appeal (to their displeasure) of a few successful megachurches whose examples provided pragmatic models for implementing this style of worship for evangelistic success. However, that mainline telling of contemporary worship's history is incomplete—like the white mainline appropriation of this form of worship—because it overlooks the Pentecostal sacramentality that lays behind the rise of contemporary worship in many critical aspects.

---

38. Matthew Sigler, "Misplacing Charisma: Where Contemporary Worship Lost Its Way," http://seedbed.com/feed/misplacing-charisma-contemporary-worship-lost-way/, accessed February 1, 2016.

Conclusion
CONTEMPORARY WORSHIP'S FUTURE

What is the future of contemporary worship? Where is it going?

As we contemplate those questions we are a bit hesitant to lay out a definitive vision for the years ahead. It is always easier—and more comfortable—for historians to speak about the past than about the future. The ground feels more stable underneath us when contemplating the past, because we have a chance to review, check, and cross-check available evidence and come to reasonable conclusions about what happened. Ask us about the past and it seems like walking on solid ground. But the future? Ask us about that, and it feels like taking a big step into a fog bank. Perhaps there will be solid ground there, but perhaps not.

Nonetheless, aware of our own caution, we conclude by offering these final thoughts about what the future of contemporary worship will hold.

What is clear is that contemporary worship is not going away. Despite the recurring posts we see on social media about the anticipated demise of this style of worship—the postings usually seem to us to be anecdotal and not based on a thorough study of any kind—contemporary worship and the changes it has brought to American Protestantism are not going away. In the 1990s in the midst of worship wars, the demise of contemporary worship was an aspiration of its opponents. Now that the wars have at least come to a truce on most battlefields, predicting its demise seems like wishful thinking at best. If anything, because of the continuing strengthening of Pentecostalism here and abroad, it might be fair to say that some form of "contemporized" worship is likely to become a dominant shape of Protestant worship across the globe.

And there is nothing that convinces us that the nine defining qualities of contemporary worship, spelled out in chapter 1, will disappear. Indeed, some have become so entrenched that they are now mundane. Their original revolutionary nature has become domesticated because of our familiarity with these qualities and their appeal to us. Using contemporary, nonarchaic

English, for example, is questioned only in the smallest liturgical outposts still committed to the King James Bible. And the growing informality in American culture generally continues to reinforce Sunday morning as a time of informality. (And, to be honest, we ourselves are happy to be free from our coats and ties on Sunday.)

In addition to the nine defining qualities, several central values that have served as the substructure for contemporary worship over the years have not waned at all. Since the 1960s intelligibility, accessibility, creativity, novelty, and, especially, authenticity have been values whose worth in worship seem to be self-evident. What is interesting to us is that, in every new round of contemporary worship, promoters write about the need for these values as if they, the promoters, are discovering these values anew.

The fact that contemporary worship will continue and its key qualities and values will stay in place does not mean there will not be changes and adaptations in the years ahead. Of course, that doesn't seem to apply to some congregations we have seen, where, after first venturing out into contemporary worship fifteen or twenty years ago, they have changed little about what they first implemented, including a song repertoire that is way out of date.

Some clouds on the horizon are prominent already. For instance, there is a retro movement in some circles. Eschewing the strong liturgical iconoclasm of some early adopters of contemporary worship, some folks have begun to wonder if there are aspects of the church year, ancient liturgical texts, sacramental life, and older, distinctive forms of liturgical architecture that might actually enhance faith, not be a hindrance to it.

We also think that advancements in technology will be an important growth edge for many congregations. The technological sophistication of contemporary worship in some circles and in some congregations will continue to follow the lead of American culture and entertainment's use of technology. We wonder if the widening gap of technological sophistication among congregations will result in an even broader range of forms of contemporary worship than exists now.

There will also continue to be advancements in music, too. Already we can see a clear interest in a hymn retuning movement in which older hymn texts are refitted with new tunes in some form of popular musical style. The words may be the same but the feel is completely different. Similarly, we see a growing interest in acoustic music making. The place where some forms of contemporary worship began seems to be where some congregations are returning: to the simple beauty of acoustic—not electronic—instruments.

And so, again, what is the future of contemporary worship? Where is it going? We may not be able to predict its precise forms in the future, but we are confident that it will be *con-temp-orary*, with-the-times. Its core qualities and defining values will continue to hold sway.

FOR FURTHER STUDY

(Note: The following bibliography is not intended as a list of how-to guides on contemporary worship. Neither is it a catalog of either its proponents or detractors. What follows is a bibliography of scholarly writings relevant to the study of the history of contemporary worship.)

Chapter 1: What Is *Contemporary Worship*?

Bains, David R. "Contemporary Worship: Trends and Patterns in Christian America." In *Faith in America: Changes, Challenges, New Directions*. Vol. 3, *Personal Spirituality Today*, edited by Charles H. Lippy. Westport, CT: Praeger, 2006.

Bergler, Thomas E. *The Juvenilization of American Christianity*. Grand Rapids: Wm. B. Eerdmans Publishing Co., 2012.

Chaves, Mark. *American Religion: Contemporary Trends*. Princeton: Princeton University Press, 2011.

Justice, Deborah R. "Sonic Change, Social Change, Sacred Change: Music and the Reconfiguration of American Christianity." PhD diss., Indiana University, 2012.

Liturgy. This journal has theme issues on contemporary worship from 2004 (vol. 19, no. 4) and 2017 (vol. 32, no. 1).

Miller, Donald E. *Reinventing American Protestantism: Christianity in the New Millennium*. Berkeley: University of California Press, 1997.

Park, Andy, Lester Ruth, and Cindy Rethmeier. *Worshiping with the Anaheim Vineyard: The Emergence of Contemporary Worship*. Grand Rapids: Wm. B. Eerdmans Publishing Co., 2017.

Plantinga, Cornelius, Jr., and Sue A. Rozeboom. *Discerning the Spirits: A Guide to Thinking about Christian Worship Today*. Grand Rapids: Wm. B. Eerdmans Publishing Co., 2003.

Redman, Robb. *The Great Worship Awakening: Singing a New Song in the Postmodern Church*. San Francisco: Jossey-Bass, 2002.

Ross, Melanie C. *Evangelical Versus Liturgical? Defying a Dichotomy*. Grand Rapids: Wm. B. Eerdmans Publishing Co., 2014.

Ruth, Lester. "Divine, Human, or Devilish? The State of the Question on the Writing of the History of Contemporary Worship." *Worship* 88, no. 4 (July 2014): 290–310.

Spinks, Bryan D. *The Worship Mall: Contemporary Responses to Contemporary Culture*. New York: Church Publishing, Inc., 2011.

Thumma, Scott. *Beyond Megachurch Myths: What We Can Learn from America's Largest Churches*. San Francisco: Jossey-Bass, 2007.

York, Terry W. *America's Worship Wars*. Peabody, MA: Hendrickson Publishers, 2003.

Chapter 2: Time in Contemporary Worship

Albrecht, Daniel E. "Worshiping and the Spirit: Transmuting Liturgy Pentecostally." In *The Spirit in Worship—Worship in the Spirit*, edited by Teresa Berger and Bryan D. Spinks. Collegeville, MN: Liturgical Press, 2009.

Connell, Martin. *Eternity Today: On the Liturgical Year*. 2 vols. New York: Continuum, 2006.

Ingalls, Monique M. "Singing Heaven Down to Earth: Spiritual Journeys, Eschatological Sounds, and Community Formation in Evangelical Conference Worship." *Ethnomusicology* 55, no. 2 (spring–summer 2011): 255–79.

Stookey, Laurence Hull. *Calendar: Christ's Time for the Church*. Nashville: Abingdon Press, 1996.

Chapter 3: The Space of Contemporary Worship

Bratton, Susan Power. *ChurchScape: Megachurches and the Iconography of Environment*. Waco, TX: Baylor University Press, 2016.

Crowley, Eileen D. *Liturgical Art for a Media Culture*. Collegeville, MN: Liturgical Press, 2007.

————. *A Moving Word: Media Art in Worship*. Minneapolis: Augsburg Fortress, 2006.

Crowley-Horak, Eileen. "Testing the Fruits: Aesthetics as Applied to Liturgical Media Art." PhD diss., Union Theological Seminary, 2002.

Fenimore, James A., Jr. "High-Tech Worship: Digital Display Technologies and Protestant Liturgical Practice in the U.S." PhD diss., Rensselaer Polytechnic Institute, 2009.

————. "High-Tech Worship: Gender Politics and the Appropriation of Multimedia Technology for Christian Worship." In *Women, Gender, and Technology*, edited by Mary Frank Fox, Deborah G. Johnson, and Sue V. Rosser, 174–92. Urbana: University of Illinois Press, 2006.

Haulk, Donnie. *God's Laws of Communication: Exploring the Physiology and Technology of Worship*. Charlotte, NC: AE Global Media, Inc., 2011.

Kilde, Jeanne Halgren. *When Church Became Theatre: The Transformation of Evangelical Architecture and Worship in Nineteenth-Century America*. New York: Oxford University Press, 2002.

Loveland, Anne C., and Otis B. Wheeler. *From Meetinghouse to Megachurch: A Material and Cultural History*. Columbia: University of Missouri Press, 2003.

Schultze, Quentin J. *High-Tech Worship? Using Presentational Technologies Wisely*. Grand Rapids: Baker Books, 2004.

White, James F., and Susan J. White. *Church Architecture: Building and Renovating for Christian Worship*. New edition. Akron, OH: OSL Publications, 1998.

Wilford, Justin G. *Sacred Subdivisions: The Postsuburban Transformation of American Evangelicalism*. New York: New York University Press, 2012.

Chapters 4 and 5: The Music of Contemporary Worship

Abbington, James, ed. *Readings in African American Church Music and Worship*. 2 vols. Chicago: GIA Publications, 2001, 2014.

Busman, Joshua Kalin. "(Re)Sounding Passion: Listening to American Evangelical Worship Music, 1997–2015." PhD diss., University of North Carolina, 2015.

Cusic, Don, ed. *Encyclopedia of Contemporary Christian Music: Pop, Rock, and Worship*. Santa Barbara, CA: Greenwood Press, 2010.

Di Sabatino, David. *The Jesus People Movement: An Annotated Bibliography and General Resource*. Westport, CT: Greenwood Press, 1999.

Eskridge, Larry. *God's Forever Family: The Jesus People Movement in America*. New York: Oxford University Press, 2013.

———. "The Praise and Worship Revolution." *Christian Today* (October 29, 2008), http://www.christianitytoday.com/history/2008/october/praise-and-worship -revolution.html.

González, Justo L. *Alabadle! Hispanic Christian Worship*. Nashville: Abingdon Press, 1996.

Hamilton, Michael S. "The Triumph of the Praise Song: How Guitars Beat Out the Organ in the Worship Wars." *Christianity Today* 43, no. 8 (July 12, 1999): 28–35. Reprinted in *Worship at the Next Level: Insight from Contemporary Voices*, edited by Tim A. Dearborn and Scott Coil. Grand Rapids: Baker Books, 2004.

Hollandsworth, Dave, comp. *Jesus Movement*. http://one-way.org/jesusmovement/.

Ingalls, Monique M. "Awesome in This Place: Sound, Space, and Identity in Contemporary North American Evangelical Worship." PhD diss., University of Pennsylvania, 2008.

———. "A New Day of Worship: Transnational Connections, Musical Meaning, and the 1990s 'British Invasion' of North American Evangelical Worship Music." In *The Oxford Handbook of Music and World Christianities*, edited by Suzel Reily and Jonathan Dueck. Oxford: Oxford University Press, 2016.

Ingalls, Monique M., Carolyn Landau, and Tom Wagner. *Christian Congregational Music: Performance, Identity and Experience*. Burlington, VT: Ashgate Publishing Co., 2013.

Ingalls, Monique M., and Amos Yong, eds. *The Spirit of Praise: Music and Worship in Global Pentecostal-Charismatic Christianity*. University Park: The Pennsylvania State University Press, 2015.

Justice, Deborah R. "Sonic Change, Social Change, Sacred Change: Music and the Reconfiguration of American Christianity." PhD diss., Indiana University, 2012.

Lim, Swee Hong. "Methodologies of Musiking in Practical Theology: Portal into the World of Contemporary Worship Song." *International Journal of Practical Theology* 18, no. 2 (2014): 305–16.

Maynard-Reid, Pedrito U. *Diverse Worship: African-American, Caribbean & Hispanic Perspectives*. Downers Grove, IL: InterVarsity Press, 2000.

Nekola, Anna E. "Between This World and the Next: The Musical 'Worship Wars' and Evangelical Ideology in the United States, 1960–2005." PhD diss., University of Wisconsin-Madison, 2009.

———. "US Evangelicals and the Redefinition of Worship Music." In *Mediating Faiths: Religion and Socio-Cultural Change in the Twenty-First Century*, edited by Michael Bailey and Guy Redden. Burlington, VT: Ashgate Publishing Co., 2011.

Nekola, Anna E., and Tom Wagner, eds. *Congregational Music-Making and Community in a Mediated Age*. Burlington, VT: Ashgate Publishing Co., 2015.

Pollard, Deborah Smith. *When the Church Becomes Your Party: Contemporary Gospel Music*. Detroit: Wayne State University Press, 2008.

Reagan, Wen. "A Beautiful Noise: A History of Contemporary Worship Music in Modern America." PhD diss., Duke University, 2015.

Riches, Tanya. "The Evolving Theological Emphasis of Hillsong Worship (1996–2007)." *Australasian Pentecostal Studies* 13 (2010): 87–133.

———. "Shout to the Lord!: Music and Change at Hillsong: 1996–2007." MPhil thesis, Australian Catholic University, 2010.

Riches, Tanya, and Tom Wagner. "The Evolution of Hillsong Music: From Australian Pentecostal Congregation into Global Brand." *Australian Journal of Communication* 39, no. 1 (June 2012): 17–36.

Scheer, Greg. "Praise & Worship, From Jesus People to Gen X." In *New Songs of Celebration Render: Congregational Song in the Twenty-First Century*, edited by C. Michael Hawn. Chicago: GIA Publications, Inc., 2013.

Ulmer, Kenneth C. "Transformational Worship in the Life of a Church." In *Worship That Changes Lives: Multidisciplinary and Congregational Perspectives on Spiritual Transformation*, edited by Alexis D. Abernethy. Grand Rapids: Baker Academic, 2008.

Chapter 6: Prayer and Contemporary Worship

Aghahowa, Brenda Eatman. *Praising in Black and White: Unity and Diversity in Christian Worship*. Cleveland, OH: United Church Press, 1996.

Brown, Patricia D. "Prayer." In *The Upper Room Dictionary of Christian Spiritual Formation*, edited by Keith Beasley-Topliffe. Nashville: Upper Room Books, 2003.

Foley, John Miles. *Oral-Formulaic Theory and Research: An Introduction and Annotated Bibliography*. New York: Garland Publishing, 1985.

Holmes, Stephen R. "Listening for the *Lex Orandi*: The Constructed Theology of Contemporary Worship Events." *Scottish Journal of Theology* 66, no. 2 (2013): 192–208.

Luhrmann, T. M. *When God Talks Back: Understanding the American Evangelical Relationship with God*. New York: Alfred A. Knopf, 2012.

Ong, Walter J. *Orality and Literacy: The Technologizing of the Word*. 3rd ed. New York: Routledge, 2013.

Saliers, Don E. "Prayer and Emotion: Shaping and Expressing Christian Life." In *Christians at Prayer*, edited by John Gallen. Notre Dame: University of Notre Dame Press, 1977.

Steven, James. "The Spirit in Contemporary Charismatic Worship." In *The Spirit in Worship—Worship in the Spirit*, edited by Teresa Berger and Bryan D. Spinks. Collegeville, MN: Liturgical Press, 2009.

Titon, Jeff Todd. *Powerhouse for God: Speech, Chant, and Song in an Appalachian Baptist Church*. Austin: University of Texas Press, 1988.

Chapter 7: The Bible and Preaching in Contemporary Worship

Abbington, James, ed. *Readings in African American Church Music and Worship*. Vol. 2. Chicago: GIA Publications, Inc., 2014.

Carroll, Jackson W. *God's Potters: Pastoral Leadership and the Shaping of Congregations*. Grand Rapids: Wm. B. Eerdmans Publishing Co., 2006.

Daniell, David. *The Bible in English: Its History and Influence*. New Haven: Yale University Press, 2003.

Phifer, Stephen R. *Worship That Pleases God: The Passion and Reason of True Worship*. Victoria, BC: Trafford, 2005, 2014.

Ruth, Lester. "How 'Pop' Are the New Worship Songs? Investigating the Levels of Popular Cultural Influence on Contemporary Worship Music." *Global Forum on Arts and Christian Faith* 3, no. 1 (2015), http://www.artsandchristianfaith.org/index.php/journal/article/view/20/19.

Stevenson, Jill. *Sensational Devotion: Evangelical Performance in Twenty-First-Century America*. Ann Arbor: The University of Michigan Press, 2013.

Webb, Joseph M. *Preaching for the Contemporary Service*. Nashville: Abingdon Press, 2006.

Wegner, Paul D. *The Journey from Texts to Translations: The Origin and Development of the Bible*. Grand Rapids: Baker Books, 1999.

Chapter 8: The Sacramentality of Contemporary Worship

Drake, Nick J. "Towards a Sacramental Understanding of Charismatic Sung Worship: The Mediation of God's Presence through Corporate Singing." MA thesis, Kings College London, 2008.

Koenig, Sarah. "This Is My Daily Bread: Toward a Sacramental Theology of Evangelical Praise and Worship." *Worship* 82, no. 2 (March 2008): 141–61.

Ruth, Lester. "A Rose by Any Other Name: Attempts at Classifying North American Protestant Worship." In *The Conviction of Things Not Seen: Worship and Ministry in the 21st Century*, edited by Todd E. Johnson. Grand Rapids: Brazos Press, 2002.

Ward, Pete. *Selling Worship: How What We Sing Has Changed the Church*. Bletchley, UK: Paternoster, 2005.

INDEX

Witt, Marcos, 81–82, 114, 130
Witvliet, John D., 122n2, 134n28
Wohlgemuth, Paul, 45n10
World Council of Churches, 115
worship (as synonymous term with music), 4, 6, 13–14
worship leader
    as term for chief musician, 6, 12, 18, 31–34, 37, 39, 49, 57, 68–69, 71, 77–78, 81, 83, 87, 92, 97–98, 100, 102–3, 108–9, 113–14, 122, 127, 129–31
    historical development as technical term, 18, 96–97, 129–31

Worship Leader (magazine), 31
Worship Times (magazine), 31
worship wars, 11–12, 20, 74, 138, 141
Wright, Jan, 11n13, 117
Wright, Timothy (Tim), 9n9, 11n13, 35, 97n10, 116, 117

youth, 5, 16–17, 22, 29, 42, 43, 57, 77, 117

Zschech, Darlene, 76–78